Wakefield Libraries & Information Services

This book should be returned by the last date stamped above. You may renew the loan personally, by post or telephone for a further period if the book is not required by another reader.

Steam Trails

Scottish Lowlands and Borders

Michael Clemens

Ian Allan
PUBLISHING

Front cover: The impressive Caledonian Railway terminus of Edinburgh Princes Street, which would later close in 1965, is seen on 5 October 1963 as No 46251 *City of Nottingham* couples up to work the 'Duchess Commemorative' rail tour back to Crewe.

Back cover: It is Easter Monday 15 April 1963 and the evening sun illuminates three residents of Stranraer shed: No 72006 *Clan Mackenzie*, Ivatt Class 2 2-6-0 No 46467 and 'Black Five' No 44795.

Previous page: The Easter 1963 series of rail tours covered the south-west of Scotland on Easter Monday, as 'Jubilee' No 45588 calls at Castle Douglas.

Right: Right: In this September 1964 photograph on the Waverley Route, one of the highest ever sustained outputs for a Gresley 'A4' is being achieved on the climb to Whitrope Summit with the 'The Scottish Lowlander' rail tour.

First published 2012

ISBN 978 0 7110 3646 8

Published by Ian Allan Publishing
an imprint of Ian Allan Publishing Ltd, Hersham, Surrey KT12 4RG

Printed in England by Ian Allan Printing Ltd, Hersham, Surrey KT12 4RG

Visit the Ian Allan website at *www.ianallanpublishing.com*

INTRODUCTION

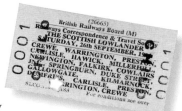

IN CHOOSING A TITLE OF 'Scottish Lowlands and Borders' for this book I was looking for something that would broadly identify with the area north from Carlisle and Newcastle upon Tyne to approximately the Forth and Clyde. The Scottish Lowlands, although a term in general usage, is not a recognised geographical area and can refer to all that part of Scotland that is not the Highlands, a definition that would include much of north-eastern Scotland such as Dundee and Aberdeen, places that are not in this book. I then came across the website of the Forestry Commission Scotland, whose Scottish Lowlands Forest District seems to correspond quite well with the north of the area I am looking to cover, but not the south of Scotland. It all seemed to get rather confusing, so perhaps appropriately for a book on railways, the deciding factor for me was the name of a rail tour that my late father and I travelled on in September 1964 together with two long-standing railway pals of ours, 'The Scottish Lowlander'. Although my child ticket No 0001 (I was 13 at the time) doesn't directly mention the Forth, the Clyde, Edinburgh or Glasgow, these were the northern limits of the trip. The 'Scottish Lowlander' rail tour is also regarded as one of the most epic in terms of locomotive performance in railway history, a place it shares with the Ian Allan high-speed 'Castle' tour from Paddington to Plymouth and back in May 1964, and a trip on which I also had the privilege of travelling. The 'Scottish Lowlander' was also thought at the time to be the last ever working of a Stanier 'Coronation' Pacific, a class regarded by many as the most powerful to run in the UK; happily, though, thanks to the preservation movement it is possible once again to see one of these fine locomotives at work.

My father's railway passion wasn't just confined to our local South Midlands area but covered the entire country, and as long as it didn't conflict with school I was generally with him. His eldest first cousin and her family moved to the old part of East Kilbride in the years after the Second World War, and her husband set up the Philips factory at Hamilton and would tell me stories of travelling to and from London on the overnight sleeper trains for business meetings, sometimes with the pioneer main-line diesels Nos 10000 and 10001. Although there were the occasional day trips by rail to Scotland from home, most of our visits would be for about a week, with East Kilbride as the base, and very often this would be at Easter to coincide with the annual 'Scottish Rambler' rail tours. Those journeys north, of 300-plus miles, would sometimes be by rail, but when done by car, before the motorway network, they seemed to take an eternity, having to go through town centres like Warrington and Wigan. How different it all is now, when for the funeral of my aunt in 2006 we travelled from Worcestershire to Clydebank Crematorium via the Erskine Bridge and back in a day.

In addition to the colour and black & white photographs we took, which appear in this book, the fast-changing railway scene from the late 1950s onwards was also being recorded by us on movie film, together

with even the sound of the locomotives on tape recorders. It is difficult to remember after so many years whether it was my father or I who took particular photos, which is why I have included a shot at Greenock Princes Pier that has my father in the corner complete with movie camera. At the time of the earlier material in this book I was a very young lad, but as the years went on I was involved directly more and more in generating our collection of railway material; however, the credit lies with my father, not me, for having the foresight to create such a wide and extensive archive of the railways of Britain and beyond.

The accompanying 1982 photograph taken at Redditch College by David Morgan, West Midlands Area Secretary of the Welshpool & Llanfair Railway, shows my father C. N. 'Jim' Clemens on the right, while on the left is the famous author on Welsh narrow gauge railways J. I. C. Boyd and his wife. Very often on our railway trips and visits friends of my father would come with us, and although my father died suddenly at work at the young age of 65 in October 1987, these old friends are now themselves passing away. I have been very fortunate in that the various widows and children of these old pals have given me permission to use their archive material in this book. Eric Parker from Worcester was a great diarist; he believed that everything should be written down, as you were likely to forget the details as the years went by, and I have used this detail in the commentaries that follow. Eric was also a Great Western man through and through. He won first prize in the on-train raffle during the September 1964 'Scottish Lowlander' tour and the choice was a biography of either Sir William Stanier or Sir Nigel Gresley; naturally he chose Sir William. Also from Worcester was Alan Maund, who independently toured the area covered in this book with his wife in the early 1960s. A number of Alan's excellent photographs, all of which are in colour, do not give the location, and it has provided some most interesting exercises for me in trying to tie them down, I hope correctly.

The book begins at Carlisle Citadel station, one of the gateways to Scotland and a focal point for Anglo-Scottish traffic, and we start our journey north up the old Caledonian Railway. Before crossing the border a visit is

Right: The main body of this book begins with the last ever pre-preservation arrival of a Stanier 'Coronation' at Carlisle on 26 September 1964, here the special train is awaiting departure from Crewe.

made to the large locomotive depot at Carlisle Kingmoor, one of the final strongholds of main-line steam and the last British Railways shed to have an allocation of more than 100 locomotives. Then it's onwards through Kirtlebridge, where the remains of the one-time Solway Junction Railway can be seen, to Lockerbie and Beattock. Civil engineer Joseph Locke, when considering whether to follow either the Annandale route or that through Nithsdale to the north for the new railway, was confronted with the problem of climbing over the southern uplands. Following initial investigations he chose Nithsdale, largely because of the difficult terrain in the final few miles to Beattock Summit, but later decided on Annandale. To keep the grade from Beattock to Beattock Summit similar to that which he already had in mind for crossing Shap Fells involved a climb of about 10 miles. The result, as we will see at Beattock, was that banking engines were required all through the steam era and beyond to help heavy trains up the grade. It is climbing to Beattock Summit that we have our first sight of Highland Railway 4-6-0 No 103; this locomotive and Caledonian Railway 4-2-2 No 123, North British Railway 4-4-0 No 256 *Glen Douglas* and Great North of Scotland Railway 4-4-0 No 49 *Gordon Highlander* were all restored

to working order in the late 1950s, and were used on special trains until 1965; all will appear in this book. Carstairs became the junction for where the Caledonian Railway's Anglo-Scottish route split, with lines to both Edinburgh and Glasgow. An important locomotive depot was built there, where in addition to active steam we see for the first time in this book something that became a familiar sight in the early 1960s, rows of stored and condemned steam locomotives awaiting their fate. The end of 1962 in particular had seen a holocaust of Scottish Region steam, with 212 locomotives being withdrawn in the last week of the year, according to the magazine of the Stephenson Locomotive Society.

Having entered Scotland along what is now often called the West Coast Main Line, we then head east over to the Tyne, George Stephenson's birthplace and a pioneering area in the development of steam locomotives; perhaps appropriately, it was once thought that the last active BR main-line steam would be in this area, but it was not to be. Main-line steam activity is seen at Tyne Dock, Gateshead and Newcastle upon Tyne, including the colourful 'J72' station pilot at Central station repainted in the old North Eastern Railway livery. In our search for steam around Britain we didn't just concentrate on main-line locomotives and ignore the industrial scene; in fact, after the demise of BR main-line steam the largest user nationally became the National Coal Board. Ashington, once considered the largest coal-mining village in the world, used to have an extensive internal system that even boasted its own passenger service. A more complete contrast to the dirt and grime seen at Ashington would be difficult to find than that of the Harton Railway, where white electric locomotives were used for coal haulage with German equipment that pre-dated the First World War. For those who have always considered industrial steam locomotives to be not the 'real thing', a visit is made to Widdrington, where a genuine LNER 'J94' is seen in immaculate condition working at the disposal point, still with its BR number and crest.

A journey into deepest rural Northumberland begins at Morpeth in November 1963 on the last train to Rothbury, Reedsmouth and the old Border Counties line. Still in Northumberland, and again in 1963, visits are made to Wooler and Coldstream, the latter station having the rare distinction of being in a different country from the town after which it was named. As mentioned above, despite the title of this book, electric traction has already been included, while at Burnmouth, again in 1963, diesel traction is seen not for the first or the last time, including the famous 'Deltic' class.

In addition to today's West and East Coast lines to Scotland, up to 1969 there also existed the Waverley Route, which connected Carlisle via Hawick and Galashiels to Edinburgh. This much-lamented line, currently being partially rebuilt thanks to the devolved Scottish Parliament, is seen

in the early 1960s, together with visits to Roxburgh, Jedburgh and Duns. Edinburgh is reached via Niddrie Junction and the rather cramped St Margarets locomotive shed, before the 1965-closed terminus at Princes Street is seen. Then both sides of the Forth are visited, including the long-dismantled branch that passed through the approach spans of the Forth Bridge to South Queensferry. Coal can be seen to be very much still king at Bathgate in 1960, before we move on to the Bonnybridge Silica & Fireclay Company, where specially constructed 'Palbrick' wagons are in use being hauled by genuine Caley steam. Few would have thought that the last work of Gresley's high-speed 'A4s' would have been on the Aberdeen to Glasgow route, but with their redundancy following dieselisation of the ECML out of London King's Cross, together with the poor performance of the locally manufactured D61xx diesels used out of Buchanan Street to Aberdeen, this is exactly what happened – steam, diesel and industrial steam are seen around Glenboig and Cumbernauld. What proved to be the most difficult of Alan Maund's slides to identify, involving days and days of research, are two attractive colour shots from around 1960 near Lennoxtown, with the Campsie Fells in the background.

At Glasgow, Queen Street and Central are covered, then St Enoch in 1959 with a rare double-heading combination of a 'Clan' and a 'Britannia'; not forgotten are the Glasgow trams, with a lovely 1960 shot that includes Alan Maund's very smart-looking Ford Consul II complete with whitewall tyres. A surprise withdrawal to many in the December 1962 mass culling of Scottish steam were the five 'Clans' based at Polmadie, and the row of forlorn 4-6-2s is seen during Easter 1963. A rather obscure railway was the Paisley & Renfrew, which was built to Scotch gauge and was for many years completely isolated from the national network; by the time of our 1965 visit, Paisley Abercorn station had a service of just one train per day, and that in one direction only. The Beith branch train is seen at Lugton in 1958, and also the completely derelict station of Auchenmade, which had lost its passenger service as early as 1932. On the other side of the Clyde one of the colourful electric 'Blue Trains' is seen in 1965, their mass withdrawal in December 1960 due

Right: At Gateshead shed in 1963 steam and diesel could be seen being serviced together, although the dirt and grime of steam did not best suit the more sensitive diesels.

to transformer explosions by then long behind them.

The area around Airdrie, Coatbridge, Motherwell and Hamilton once possessed a maze of railways feeding many industrial sites such as collieries and ironworks. At Whifflet the R. B. Tennent foundry employed Sentinel-type engines, which ended up as the final commercially operated steam locomotives in Scotland. It was also an area that cut up the numerous withdrawn surplus BR steam locomotives, and included the visually very memorable dump at Carnbroe, Airdrie; then working steam is seen on shed at Hamilton and Motherwell. Subsidence from old mine workings was a problem for the railways throughout this district, but perhaps not more so than at Bothwell on the NBR line to Hamilton; electrification was proposed in 1951 but the line was closed a year later due to viaduct subsidence. As East Kilbride was often our base the branch from Glasgow is seen, and also that from High Blantyre to Strathaven through the strangely named station of Quarter, and at Whitsun 1959 visits are also made to Lanark, Ponfeigh and Coalburn.

The south-west of Scotland has not been mentioned so far, and that is now remedied. This was largely Glasgow & South Western Railway territory, but we start in glorious spring sunshine at Shieldhill with the bushes budding, on the old Caledonian Railway branch from Lockerbie. Dumfries shed is host to the final LMS 2P 4-4-0 to work

in Scotland; at withdrawal it was the last of this once very common wheel arrangement on the entire British Railways system. Dumfries was also the start of the 'Port Road' to Stranraer, and the route is covered in some detail during visits in 1963 and 1965; Castle Douglas, Kirkcudbright, New Galloway, lonely Loch Skerrow and Newton Stewart, together with an aerial view dating from 80 or so years ago, are all included. Interestingly, the term 'Port Road' derives from Portpatrick, the original destination for this route but still in use many decades later, even though Portpatrick Harbour was formally abandoned in favour of Stranraer in the 1870s. The old Wigtownshire Railway south from Newton Stewart to the most southerly station in Scotland at Whithorn had always intrigued me, even more so the short branch to Garlieston that had lost its passenger service more than a century ago, and on which normal passenger stock was prohibited by 1963. A stop is made at Dunragit where there is photographic detail aplenty of this delightful country station, the goods yard even

book at lonely Barrhill, with the sun setting on a glorious 1963 spring evening across the bleak moorlands, the cause of such massive financial problems for the Girvan & Portpatrick Railway.

Looking a little more closely at items other than the still photographs we recorded at the time, all through the book are selections of tickets, some of which are from special rail tours, while others are examples from our journeys on service trains. My father would often ask at booking offices if there were any tickets that could be bought

including an original G&SWR six-wheel coach that was still in use, and thanks to the archivist of the Glasgow & South Western Railway Association a detailed line drawing of this relic from a bygone era is also included. At Stranraer both the Town station and shed are visited, while at the Harbour station is seen both the TSS *Caledonian Princess* and one of the half-cab DMUs introduced to the route from Glasgow in 1959. Then it is north to Hurlford shed (Kilmarnock), followed by Mauchline, Muirkirk, Cumnock (A&C), Annbank and Ayr before a look at the NCB system around Waterside Colliery near Dalmellington; those expecting a dirty industrial landscape will be very pleasantly surprised at the delightful rural scenery here. Finally, it is on to Girvan, then the conclusion of the

reasonably cheaply, especially if they were old or the line was about to close, just to add to the collection; perhaps the strangest was a striking deep red 1965 dog return ticket valid for a 6-mile distance from Dunragit at a cost of 1 shilling. Our entire collection of over 1,000 tickets is now viewable on my website.

A few years ago I put about sixty 1960s train tape recordings we did on my website – www.michaelclemensrailways.co.uk – and if you click on the 'Sound Bites' section you can access a list of the actual recordings. Many are of broadcast quality and I am aware of radio stations that have used them; all are freely downloadable and two relate to this book – at Mauchline and near Girvan in 1966. The movie film collection that dates from 1959 is

Right: Near Glenboig was Bedlay colliery, the last site in Scotland to use conventional steam locomotives on a commercial basis; Nos 9 & 17 bask in the May 1978 sunshine.

thought to be the largest of its type in Britain; over the last 15 years it has gradually been, and continues to be, released on DVD and VHS. With the obvious exception of the Alan Maund photographs, generally speaking there was movie film taken at the same time as the still photographs, with the Scottish movie material now released on three separate volumes. I would thoroughly recommend them to anyone who would like to see more of the areas covered in this book; all have an authentic soundtrack added, together with an informative commentary. Picking out just one movie sequence, the ascent to Whitrope Summit with 'A4' No 60007 on the 'Scottish Lowlander' tour, with one of the highest ever sustained power outputs being developed by the class, looks very impressive. They can be purchased via the Ian Allan website or by following the links in the DVD & Video section of my website mentioned above.

The photographs that follow in this book mainly cover the period from 1958 and through the 1960s to the end of British Railways main-line steam, and in the case of some of the industrial steam as late as 1978, the majority of the photographs having been taken between 1958 and 1966. It is largely a vanished world, as many of the locations visited are no longer on the railway map, while of course regular BR main-line steam finally came to an end nationally around Lancashire in August 1968. In Scotland the last steam diagrams were scheduled to cease from 1 May 1967, but steam continued to penetrate from the still open steam depot at Carlisle Kingmoor, sometimes quite deeply. The 20.32 passenger working from Carlisle to Perth carried on regularly diagrammed with steam until early June, and even in December 1967, the last month that Kingmoor was open, steam was seen at Ayr, Polmadie and Motherwell. From 1968, however, the only steam locomotives noted were withdrawn ones and destined for the cutter's torch, such as five arrivals at Motherwell shed on 20 January.

I hope you enjoy this book of railways in years gone by, but don't forget that the outlook for Scottish railways today and in the future looks very positive. Devolved government has proved a boon for the railways of Scotland, with considerable investment in the system: railways are being put back, such as Bathgate to Airdrie and the Waverley Route to Tweedbank, double track has been restored, as from Lugton towards Kilmarnock, more electrification is proposed, and there is a general expansion of services together with the prospect of more to come in future years – long may it continue.

Michael Clemens
PERSHORE, WORCESTERSHIRE
AUGUST 2010

Left: Crowds gather around 'Coronation' No 46256 *Sir William A. Stanier, F.R.S.* on 26 September 1964 as it comes off the 'Scottish Lowlander' tour with what was the last ever pre-preservation arrival at Carlisle of one of these impressive locomotives. It has been said that this tour (together with the Ian Allan high-speed 'Castle' run from Paddington to Plymouth and back in May 1964) was one of the most epic in railway history in terms of locomotive performance. On its way north to Carlisle climbing Shap, No 46256 developed an equivalent drawbar horsepower (edbhp) of 2,400 for a short time. Going back south to Crewe, a 13-minutes-late departure from Carlisle on a dark rainy night gave the incentive for a net time of 38¾ minutes to Shap Summit with a 450-ton load. After arrival back at Crewe, the locomotive's fire was dropped and No 46256 never moved again until it went for scrap with, so it was rumoured, the rail tour reporting number still in place; so passed the 'Coronation' Pacifics.

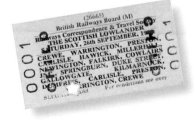

Above: The north end of Carlisle Citadel finds very well-presented 'Jubilee' No 45588 *Kashmir*, allocated to Carlisle Kingmoor (12A) at this time. It is Easter Monday, 15 April 1963, and *Kashmir* is hauling the 'Scottish Rambler No 2 Joint Easter Rail Tour', due to depart at 9.00am. Carlisle, the county town of Cumberland, was a focal point for Anglo-Scottish traffic, and prior to 1923 seven independent railway companies used the joint Citadel station: Caledonian, North British, North Eastern, Midland, London & North Western, Maryport & Carlisle and Glasgow & South Western. While all the companies used the one passenger station, for freight each company had at least one independent or joint goods station and marshalling yard. There used to be extensive goods lines connecting them and bypassing the passenger station, which rarely used to see goods trains as a result, probably just as well considering the limited accommodation at Citadel.

Left: Ivatt Class 2 2-6-0 No 46426 from Carlisle Upperby shed (12B), complete with a damaged chimney, is simmering away in Collier Lane sidings at the south end of Carlisle Citadel on Good Friday, 8 April 1966. This light-axleload design, together with the 2-6-2 tank engine equivalent, was quite revolutionary when it first appeared just after the Second World War. Very often new heavier designs took over from older lightweight locomotives on the main routes, the older locomotives then being reassigned to secondary lines. A local case in point was the Cockermouth, Keswick & Penrith Railway, which up to the 1950s used LNWR 'Cauliflower' 0-6-0s that dated from the 1880s, displaced from main-line service years previously. Bristling with features to improve performance and reduce maintenance costs, the Ivatt 2-6-0s were a popular and well-liked class, a world apart from the old 'Cauliflowers'. In the Lake District they were affectionately referred to as 'Penrith Lizzies', in tribute to their haulage potential on steep and curving routes that could not take the heavier locomotives.

(26020)
Stephenson Locomotive Society
(Midland Area)
Pacific Pennine Three Summits Rail Tour
SUNDAY, 12th JULY, 1964

0262   0267

Birmingham (New Street), Wolverhampton
(High Level), Shap Summit, Carlisle
(Kingmoor SK. ..s), Aisgill Summit, Leeds
(City), Standedge Summit, Stalybridge,
Stockport, Crewe, Wolverhampton (High
Level) and Birmingham (New Street)

SECOND CLASS   For conditions see over

Above: Green-liveried 'Coronation' No 46255 *City of Hereford* stands adjacent to Carlisle Kingmoor shed (12A) on the occasion of the 'Pacific Pennine Three Summits Rail Tour' on 12 July 1964; No 46255 will haul the special over the Settle & Carlisle route to Leeds. The whole train arrived from Birmingham outside the depot behind No 46251, and tour participants were allowed to wander around the shed at will, even on the main line, something unthinkable in today's health-&-safety-conscious world. Kingmoor became a stronghold of steam in its last years, redundancy elsewhere bringing in previously rare types such as Western Region 2-10-0s. It was the last steam shed in Carlisle and was also the last steam shed on the whole of the BR system to have an allocation of more than 100 locomotives, even in 1967, its last year. The author visited the depot on 15 October 1967 when there were still 118 locomotives present, 56 of them 'Black Fives'; it closed on 1 January 1968.

Above: Kingmoor, originally Etterby, was the Caledonian Railway shed at Carlisle, the Kingmoor name coming about following a major rebuilding during the First World War. This well-laid-out shed with little site restriction moved to pre-eminence in Carlisle and absorbed other depots: first the G&SWR engines at Currock, then aspects of Durran Hill, Waverley Route duties following the closure of Canal in 1963, and finally Upperby in 1966. On Sunday 12 July 1964 there were 93 locomotives present according to Eric Parker's diaries, and prominent here are 'Britannia' No 70002 *Geoffrey Chaucer* and 'V2' No 60955. The total was made up of eight '43xxxs', five 4F 0-6-0s, 37 'Black Fives', a 'Patriot', six 'Jubilees' (including rebuilt No 45736), three 'Royal Scots', three 'Coronations', four 'Jintys', three 8Fs, an 'A1', two 'A2s', a 'V2', a 'B1', seven 'Britannias', a 'Clan', two '73xxxs' and finally eight 9Fs (including one just transferred from the Western Region).

Above: Taken from a moving train at Kirtlebridge between Carlisle and Lockerbie on 8 May 1959, during a journey from Wolverhampton to Carstairs, this picture shows what was left at the northern end of the one-time Solway Junction Railway, perhaps the most ambitious of the Anglo-Scottish railway schemes. By the early 1860s 100,000 tons of iron ore were being sent from the West Cumberland hematite mines to Scotland. To avoid Carlisle involved bridging the Solway and building a 25½-mile railway from Brayton to here at Kirtlebridge. The Solway Viaduct was more than a mile long and took 3½ years to build at a cost of about £100,000; it opened for goods in 1869. Major problems with the viaduct occurred in the winter of 1880/81 when massive chunks of ice slammed into it and 45 piers together with 37 girders collapsed. It was repaired, but the iron ore traffic declined and the viaduct was declared unsafe in 1921; traffic then ceased, with the viaduct being dismantled in 1934/35. The section between Kirtlebridge and Annan carried on as a through route until 1931.

Above: Looking north at Lockerbie on 15 April 1963, straight ahead is the main line via Beattock Summit, but No 45588 *Kashmir* will bear left on to the Caledonian branch to Dumfries. In 1835 the Grand Junction Railway, the first trunk railway in England, was looking for a route through southern Scotland to both Glasgow and Edinburgh. There were two contenders, Nithsdale or Annandale, and Joseph Locke, chief surveyor of the GJR, made preliminary surveys. Locke initially came down in favour of the less direct Nithsdale route, presumably reaching Edinburgh via Glasgow. Two people in particular queried this: the MP for Dumfriesshire, and Charles Stewart, factor for the Annandale Estates. Stewart said that the shorter Annandale route via Beattock and Upper Clydesdale could be regarded as a spear from the south that became a trident, the three prongs going left to Glasgow, right to Edinburgh and straight on to Stirling, Perth and the north. Eventually the Annandale route won and opened through Lockerbie in 1847. However, the Nithsdale route was also opened shortly after.

Left: 'Black Five' No 44702 is arriving from the south at Beattock on 2 June 1965, displaying the lamp code for an express freight train on which the automatic vacuum brake is operative on not less than 20% of the vehicles. Civil engineer Joseph Locke eventually settled on this route from Carlisle northwards to Glasgow and Edinburgh as it was the shortest, even though it involved a long and steep gradient up to Beattock Summit. His reasoning was that short routes could be finished more quickly, with less capital costs, and start earning revenue sooner; it became known as the 'up and over' school of engineering, but a consequence of this policy is seen on the right. The climb from Beattock station to Beattock Summit is 10 miles long with gradients as steep as 1 in 69, which meant that all during the steam era banking engines, like the one on the right, had to be available 24 hours a day to help push heavy loads up the bank. *A. Maund*

Right: Although the 9F 2-10-0 heavy freight locomotives regularly worked to Carlisle from Birmingham after the spring of 1957, it was not until May/June 1964 that several of the class were first allocated to Carlisle Kingmoor (12A); by 1 January 1967 the allocation had reached 24. With somebody on the right seemingly tending his allotment, No 92110 is seen arriving at Beattock on 2 June 1965 for banking assistance. This locomotive was a newcomer to Kingmoor, having arrived only on 22 May from Newton Heath, Manchester; perhaps that explains the painted 12A shed code instead of the usual cast-iron plate. Among the first duties for the Carlisle-allocated 9Fs were these limestone workings from Hardendale Quarry, Shap, to the steel plant at Ravenscraig near Motherwell; this train has the same lamp code as the previous 'Black Five' photograph. No 92110 received a heavy intermediate repair at Crewe Works from 19 April to 26 May 1966, but this did not stop withdrawal at the end of 1967 when steam finished at Kingmoor. *A. Maund*

Right: It is not surprising that D1843, heading south through Beattock on 2 June 1965, looks in pristine condition – it had entered traffic only on 21 May, having been built at Crewe. It has the original livery of dual (or two-tone) green (BR Green/ Sherwood Green) with a small yellow warning panel and red buffer beam. These Brush Type 4s were built in quantity, 512 eventually, and became the BR 'standard' in the Type 4 power category of 2,000-2,750bhp, despite having been ordered straight from the drawing board to meet BR's obsessive rush for dieselisation. D1843 was renumbered 47193 in April 1974 and carried on in service until August 2000, when it suffered a major generator fire, after which it was stored before being dispatched in December 2004 to C. F. Booth's scrapyard in Rotherham. Beattock station was still open at this time, but closed on 3 January 1972; today there is just one station open, at Lockerbie, in the 73½ miles between Carlisle and Carstairs. *A. Maund*

Left: For the Scottish Industries Exhibition held in the Kelvin Hall, Glasgow, during September 1959, four Scottish pre-Grouping veteran locomotives were restored to working order. A fifth working veteran, GWR *City of Truro* of 100mph fame, was also sent north to the exhibition, following which the four Scottish locomotives were often used on special trains around the country. This is Highland Railway 4-6-0 No 103 climbing the upper reaches of Beattock Bank on Sunday 17 October 1965. This class was notable as being the first of the 4-6-0 wheel arrangement to run in the British Isles. Introduced in 1894, the six coupled wheels gave plenty of adhesion – very useful for the Highlands – and 4-6-0s continued to be built for use in Britain up to 1957, the last country in the world to construct this type of locomotive (with Swindon producing the final example). The view here today is very different – the hillside behind the train has been partly cut away to make way for the A74(M) motorway. This was HR103's last outing as a working locomotive, as it then took up residency in the Glasgow Museum of Transport, the only surviving former Highland Railway locomotive.

Left: Joseph Locke's initial probing investigations of the Annandale route went well until he reached this area, the final three miles of the ascent to Beattock Summit. He found it such a steep and sustained ascent through countryside so rough and bleak that he turned back and made a survey of Nithsdale instead. As already explained, he eventually settled on this Annandale route, but the gradient here had to commence as far back as Beattock village if it was not to exceed the grade he already had in mind for crossing Shap Fells; even so, the bank would be more than twice as long. In July 1963 BR Standard Class 5 No 73148, allocated to Glasgow St Rollox shed (65B) for all its life, seems to be working pretty much flat out on the final section to Beattock Summit. No 73148 was one of 30 of this class of 172 fitted with the British-Caprotti valve gear, which was likely to have become the standard had steam development continued. *A. Maund*

Right: 'Jubilee' No 45698 *Mars*, allocated to Bank Hall shed at Liverpool (27A), is descending Beattock Bank in 1960. The 'Jubilees' were one of the first designs by William Stanier for the LMS after he had moved from the GWR, and he had brought two boxes of GWR drawings with him. The LMS 3B boiler used on the 'Jubilees' closely resembled in side elevation the GWR No 8 as used on the 'Castles', in particular that as revised after the first 60 'Castle' boilers. The unusual figure for water space at foundation ring level of 3¾ inches was used on only one other class, the 'Castles'; boiler dimensions were similar, the general shape of the firebox was similar, with many of the radii being identical, and there were many other points of similarity. One major difference was steaming ability, where the 'Jubilees' were weaker and, despite much effort to cure the problem, including the use of Rugby Testing Station in 1956, a class-wide solution was never implemented. *A. Maund*

Left: Despite looking rather unkempt and having a 'Not to be Moved' notice attached, CR 3F 0-6-0 No 57608 would not be withdrawn until December 1962, eight months after this photograph was taken on Kodak Ektachrome film. The location is Carstairs, which when the railway first arrived had been thought of as no more than an isolated country junction with trains running through; instead, carriages from Edinburgh and later Perth were joined at Carstairs to those from Glasgow. By the early 1850s it also became clear that pilot engines were often necessary for the long southbound climb of Beattock, thus an important depot came about. The shed seen here dates from a comprehensive remodelling that began at the end of 1934 and continued in 1935. The previous shed was not well thought of, being described variously as 'dilapidated', 'a very rough and ready structure' and 'only grease and soot held it up'! Coded 66E in 1962, it closed to steam at the end of 1966, the corrugated sheet building lasting until the 1980s.

Right: The last days of the Caledonian Railway 0-4-4Ts were fast approaching by the time of this Easter 1962 photograph, the *Railway Observer* noting only three at work in that April. No 55189, seen here at Carstairs, in fact continued in use until the end of the year, still being seen on general shunting duties in December. The end of 1962 saw a holocaust of Scottish Region steam, with 231 locomotives being withdrawn according to *The Railway Magazine*; this included No 55189, which was the last CR 0-4-4T in regular use. The class was thus rendered extinct and many regretted the passing of these handsome locomotives, although No 55189 had been disfigured by the fitting of a stovepipe chimney in place of the shapely McIntosh original. It was not the end for No 55189, though, due to the efforts of the Scottish Railway Preservation Society. A price of £750 was asked by BR to save No 55189 and, thanks to a generous donation from Mr W. E. C. Watkinson, a Worcestershire farmer, it was rescued for posterity.

Left: An unexpected sight at Carstairs shed during Easter 1965 was Thompson 'A2/3' Pacific No 60522 *Straight Deal*; it has the yellow diagonal stripe across the cab side to prohibit running south of Crewe over the AC electrified lines from September 1964. The usual work of this class was on the East Coast Main Line, but they had been an early target for withdrawal. Of the 15 class members, all had been withdrawn by June 1963 except three, including No 60522, which survived as they had all had recent overhauls. During overhaul the top lamp iron was lowered, which entailed replacing the single handrail by two short ones on either side. An agreement was reached with the Scottish Region whereby the three 'A2/3s' were exchanged for three of its own Pacifics, which it was on the point of condemning. They all ended up at Polmadie shed (66A), primarily to 'see out mileage' before withdrawal, and languished out of action for much of the time; all three were withdrawn during 1965.

Right: Carstairs was an important triangular junction that gave an impression of curving and sweeping lines everywhere, and there was plenty of space for odd sidings where locomotives could be stored. The slight bank from which this Easter 1962 photograph was taken was the original coal stage track dating from before the rebuilding of Carstairs shed; the LMS replaced it with a mechanical coaling plant. The location is to the east of the depot, the signalling in the background controlling the Edinburgh lines. No 55261 is a post-Grouping development of the CR McIntosh Class 439 standard passenger 0-4-4T, still with its shapely McIntosh chimney. Withdrawal came in the two weeks ending 7 October 1961 from Carstairs (66E). No 57451 is a CR 'Jumbo' 2F 0-6-0, withdrawn at the same time from 66E. Third in the row, 'WD' 2-10-0 No 90768 was still in capital stock at this time, withdrawal coming in July, again from 66E. At the rear is an unidentified CR McIntosh 3F 0-6-0.

Left: Happier days for 0-4-4T No 55261 as it shunts a carriage at Carstairs in the sunshine on 8 May 1959, photographed from the station platform. The original design of McIntosh 0-4-4T for the Caledonian Railway was introduced in 1895 as the '19' class, followed by the '92' class, built between 1897 and 1900, originally all with condensing apparatus for use on the Glasgow Central Low Level lines. There were variations of the final class of these handsome CR tank engines, as pictured here, which were first introduced in 1900: the '439' class, the 'Modified 439' class from 1915, the '431' class with a cast-iron front buffer beam for banking at Beattock, dating from 1922, and finally the 'Developed 439' class after the Grouping, which included No 55261. The post-Grouping engines were built with shorter chimneys, but latterly some interchange occurred. All performed well on branch, suburban and carriage pilot work, with most surviving until BR days, then closures and dieselisation gradually rendered them redundant.

Right: It is Easter 1965 and, as the author's family friend Denis Bath looks on, 'Patriot' No 45531 *Sir Frederick Harrison* manoeuvres at Carstairs shed, looking very grimy and without a nameplate, its diagonal yellow cabside warning stripe hardly visible. No 45531 had been rebuilt from its original parallel boiler condition in 1947 with a Class 2A tapered boiler as fitted to the rebuilt 'Royal Scots', to which the rebuilt 'Patriots' were then visually and performance-wise nearly identical. In 1944 the LMS decided that it needed 91 locomotives of this Class 6 power level, to be made up of 71 rebuilt 'Royal Scots', including No 46170 with the unique Class 2 boiler, and two rebuilt 'Jubilees'. This left a need for just 18 more, which is why it was only this number of 'Patriots' that were ever rebuilt; 100 boilers were constructed to cover the 91 locomotives, 99 of them being Class 2A. By 1965 there were only three rebuilt 'Patriots' left in service, all being withdrawn during the year.

Below and right: Where better to begin our journey north from the Tyne than at Tyne Dock MPD (52H), although it's a pity about the weather. On Good Friday, 8 April 1966 the author and his father travelled from Carlisle to Newcastle by rail, then by taxi to visit this shed; at the time it was being postulated, wrongly as it transpired, that the last working BR main-line steam would be in the North East. 'Q6' 0-8-0 No 63431 is underneath the locomotive hoist, the general conditions typical of the run-down facilities that BR steam had to endure during its last years. Inside the shed in the dry is one of the ten 9F 2-10-0s allocated to Tyne Dock, specifically for the dedicated iron-ore trains to Consett ironworks and fitted with air pumps to work the special wagons. No 92097 was one of the second batch of three built in 1956, and its air pumps are visible about half-way along the running board above the wheels. The iron-ore workings went over to diesel operation later that year and No 92097 was withdrawn in October. On arrival back at Newcastle Central the author and his father travelled up to Glasgow to film the Easter 1966 enthusiasts' specials; by this time the author was not under 14 years of age so should not have been travelling on a child's ticket!

Above: Great North of Scotland Railway No 49 *Gordon Highlander* has just arrived at Auchengray on 16 October 1965, tour participants are starting to pour out of the special train, and the locomotive will soon be topping up its water supply. Auchengray is on the CR route from Carstairs to Edinburgh that dates from 1848, and is now electrified, allowing East Coast Main Line services to run through to Glasgow Central. The 4-4-0 was a popular choice of wheel arrangement with the GNSR for hauling both passenger and freight services, the company having no 0-6-0 tender locomotives. The GNSR's final development was this 'F' class, later LNER 'D40', and eight locomotives were built after the First World War. No 49 was kept in first-class order as it also hauled the Royal Train from Aberdeen to Ballater (for Balmoral Castle). Withdrawn in 1958, it was one of the four Scottish pre-Grouping veteran locomotives restored to working order for the Scottish Industries Exhibition held in September 1959.

63431

23

Left: The author's family holiday in 1963 was two weeks at Scarborough, and on the middle Saturday, 24 August, a visit was made to Newcastle. The view here is of 'Q6' No 63399, another Tyne Dock-allocated locomotive, heading east by the side of Gateshead shed (52A). No 63399 is an outside-cylinder 0-8-0, a rare combination to somebody from Worcestershire but an extremely successful class, the design having been introduced in 1913 by the North Eastern Railway. The 'Q6' class, together with the 'J27' 0-6-0s also introduced by the NER, were the oldest working main-line steam designs left on the whole of BR when the last was withdrawn in September 1967. Visible on the shed are two English Electric Type 4s and a 'Peak', in amongst the dirt and grime of steam locomotives, which didn't best suit the more sensitive diesels. The first English Electric to arrive here was D237 on 16 October 1959 for East Coast Main Line services; the 'Peak' has probably worked in from Bristol or the Midlands on the NE/SW route.

Right: Also photographed on 24 August 1963 is 'A3' No 60062 *Minoru*, nearly 200 miles away from its home depot of New England, Peterborough (34E). The curve behind No 60062 leads to the King Edward VII Bridge and Newcastle Central station, and the track in front leads to Gateshead depot, from where *Minoru* appears to have come as its tender is piled high with coal; just visible in the background is a lightweight diesel shunter. Although steam had been displaced from most weekday expresses along the East Coast Main Line at this time, it was a different matter on summer Saturdays like this; the majority of the extra trains seen that day to cater for holidaymakers were still steam-hauled. The *Railway Observer* noted that Gateshead was short of steam in August 1963, with locomotives from distant sheds being appropriated. Peterborough was as far as steam normally worked down the ECML at this time – the final scheduled steam working at London King's Cross had been on Sunday 16 June 1963.

Right: 'J72' No 68736 was something of a celebrity locomotive. It had been repainted by BR in North Eastern Railway fully lined green livery at Darlington Works in May 1960, and in addition to the BR crest on its side it also has the NER one. It is seen at Newcastle Central on station pilot duties on 24 August 1963, and is having its 690-gallon tanks filled up by an ordinary hose instead of at a water column. No 68736 had originally been the station pilot at York, and still has a York shed plate (50A), even though allocated to Gateshead. Sister locomotive No 68723 also had the same livery applied by BR and it too was at Newcastle. One member of the class, No 69023, survived into preservation; now named *Joem*, it has also been repainted in the style of No 68736 and, following expiry of its boiler certificate in 1996, is currently being restored at Darlington.

Left: This is Ashington in Northumberland, at one time considered to be the world's largest coal-mining village, but, as in other parts of the country, the deep coal-mining industry here declined, and the colliery, opened in 1867, closed in 1988. The National Coal Board operated a very large internal railway system around Ashington, which at one time even boasted a passenger service. This photograph dates from March 1969 and shows No 43, an outside-cylinder 0-6-0 saddle tank built locally by Robert Stephenson & Hawthorns Ltd in 1956 with the works number 7769. It looks in terrible external condition and is coupled to some internal-use NCB wagons. A possible reason for the poor condition can just be seen in the haze to the rear of the wagons; starting in 1968, a number of the BR Class 14 diesel-hydraulic 0-6-0s were purchased for use here, no fewer than 19 of the class eventually spending time at Ashington.

Left: If Ashington was typified by dirty steam locomotives, then a more complete contrast would be difficult to find than that of the Harton Railway around South Shields, which used white electric locomotives, as seen in March 1970. The system had been electrified as early as 1908 and was the first such scheme carried out by a colliery company in Britain. It had very sharp curves where only short-wheelbase engines could be used, and gradients of up to 1 in 28. The replacement of steam by electric Bo-Bo locomotives like No 9, illustrated here, almost doubled the amount of wagons that could be taken. Note the very low height of the locomotive compared to the wagon to which it is coupled. As much of the system was in a built-up area it reduced the amount of noise, smoke and dirt caused by the coal trains. The electrical equipment and locomotives were purchased from Germany, where several electric colliery systems already existed, and the AEG name can be seen on No 9. The Harton Electric Railway ceased operations in 1989.

Right: The author's father travelled up from the Midlands to Newcastle, using the through sleeper and mail train service that started from Bristol, in order to join the 'Wansbeck Wanderer' tour of Saturday 9 November 1963. This is the scene at Morpeth after arrival from Newcastle. Ivatt Class 4 2-6-0 No 43129 of Darlington shed (51A) will now run round the train for departure due west on to the Wansbeck Railway, which had opened to Scotsgap on 23 July 1862. Up to 1872, when the line was diverted to this station, Wansbeck services had to reverse into the Blythe & Tyne station in Morpeth. After nationalisation in 1948, rather than build new designs, 110 locomotives of LMS ancestry were built for the Eastern and North Eastern Regions including No 43129. One hundred of them were built at Darlington and Doncaster between 1950 and 1952; No 43129 was one of the ten that were not, being built at Horwich.

2nd - PRIVATE DAY EXCURSION
(S.T. M2035)
SATURDAY, 9th NOVEMBER, 1963
RCTS & SLS—Joint Tours Committee
N.E.R. RAIL TOUR
Newcastle on Tyne (Central)
via Morpeth, Reedsmouth, Bellingham,
Scotsgap, Rothbury to
Newcastle on Tyne (Central)
For conditions see over

0334

0334

Right: The Wansbeck Railway Company, named after the River Wansbeck, which the railway follows, was authorised by Act of Parliament on 8 August 1859, and in July 1863 amalgamated with the North British Railway. There was no initial physical connection with the rest of the NBR system – that had to wait until the line between here at Scotsgap and Reedsmouth Junction was completed in May 1865 (Scotsgap station was originally spelled 'Scot's Gap' from opening until October 1903). These two views were both taken from the B6343 road bridge; the first, looking east, shows the station and yard. Scotsgap became a junction with the opening of the Northumberland Central Railway to Rothbury on 17 October 1870. The view to the west, which appears to show double track, is in fact two single lines, to Reedsmouth Junction on the left and to Rothbury on the right, the physical junction of the tracks being here at the station; also just visible beneath undergrowth is the track to a small turntable. No 43129 is running round the 'Wansbeck Wanderer' tour of 9 November 1963 before travelling along the Rothbury branch. The North Eastern Railway had running powers to here from Morpeth, which it exercised once a week for livestock traffic. For many years three passenger trains ran daily (except Sundays) in each direction from Rothbury though Scotsgap to Morpeth, and the same number between Reedsmouth Junction and Scotsgap, all passengers to and from the Reedsmouth direction having to change trains at Scotsgap. The last regular passenger trains ran on Saturday 13 September 1952, and Scotsgap closed completely on and from Monday 3 October 1966.

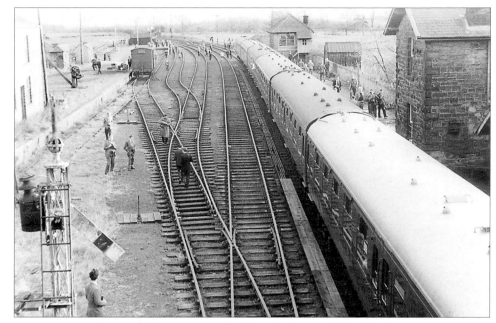

Left: Rothbury became generally recognised as a health resort in Victorian times, and by 1911 its population was 1,147. The original 1863 Act envisioned the Northumberland Central constructing a 49¾-mile railway from Scotsgap to Cornhill (Coldstream); however, the section north of Rothbury was abandoned by a subsequent Act of 1867, its place largely being taken by the NER line north from Alnwick. The arrival of the six-coach 'Wansbeck Wanderer' hauled by a 2-6-0 created something of a problem at Rothbury, as this turntable was only long enough for 0-6-0s, latterly the 'J27s'. The train had to be backed out of the station and split in two to enable No 43129 to get to the other end, before reassembling it. Regular passenger services had ceased in 1952 and the line was totally closed on and from Monday 11 November 1963, two days after this trip. Many local residents came to see this final passenger train departure and in the afternoon sunshine it left to the sound of a Northumbrian pipe band.

Right: The 'Wansbeck Wanderer' is now seen at Reedsmouth, popularly called Reedsmouth Junction and spelled differently from the nearby village of Redesmouth. The right-hand line went east to Morpeth and that to the left north for Hawick, both routes combining here to head south to Hexham. The NBR, anxious to reach Tyneside from Scotland, saw the 42-mile-long Border Counties Railway from near Hexham northwards through Reedsmouth to Riccarton as a means of achieving this. The BCR purchased enough land for double track but traffic never really developed, and a single track sufficed throughout the entire history of the line. The station building here was unusual in that it was surmounted by a water tank holding more than 60,000 gallons. Just north of the station on the Hawick route was an engine shed, which closed in 1952. By this time, 9 November 1963, the line south to Hexham had already been closed and lifted, and the only traffic was freight from the Morpeth direction north to Bellingham; complete formal closure came two days later.

Left: After 1968 the largest operator of steam locomotives in the country was the National Coal Board, but some enthusiasts never thought of the NCB locomotives as 'proper' ones. The best of both worlds could be found at Widdrington Disposal Point, operated by Derek Crouch (Contractors) Ltd on behalf of the National Coal Board Opencast Executive. The site was 8½ miles north of Morpeth and linked to the East Coast Main Line by a mile-long branch. Standing by the locomotive shed in March 1969 and looking in excellent condition is an 'Austerity' tank built by Andrew Barclay in 1946, works number 2212. This was actually a genuine LNER Class 'J94', one of 75 purchased from the Ministry of Supply in 1946 and still carrying its BR number of 68078, in addition to Derek Crouch's number L2; also visible is a faded BR crest above the BR number. In BR days No 68078 spent much time at Immingham, but was withdrawn from Langwith Junction in 1963 before purchase for use here, after which it was preserved.

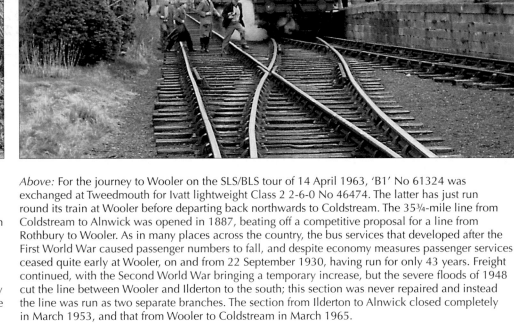

Above: Another contrast to the usual NCB-operated industrial railway was that connecting Shilbottle Colliery, south of Alnmouth, to the East Coast Main Line. No 48 is making its way up the steeply graded 1½-mile-long branch to the colliery through pleasant open countryside in March 1970. The colliery had been purchased by the Co-operative Wholesale Society (CWS) in the early 20th century and became the only pit in the area where workers were given a week's holiday with pay and also enjoyed a pension scheme. The coal from Shilbottle Colliery was very highly regarded; according to Hansard, the wife of Jo Grimond (one-time MP for Orkney & Shetland and leader of the Liberal Party) said that her coalman in the Orkney Islands used to occasionally appear with a look of triumph on his face and say, 'I've got you some Shilbottle coal, Mrs Grimond,' such was the reputation of the coal. Shilbottle Colliery was connected underground to nearby Whittle Colliery in 1978, and rail traffic then ceased.

Above: For the journey to Wooler on the SLS/BLS tour of 14 April 1963, 'B1' No 61324 was exchanged at Tweedmouth for Ivatt lightweight Class 2 2-6-0 No 46474. The latter has just run round its train at Wooler before departing back northwards to Coldstream. The 35¾-mile line from Coldstream to Alnwick was opened in 1887, beating off a competitive proposal for a line from Rothbury to Wooler. As in many places across the country, the bus services that developed after the First World War caused passenger numbers to fall, and despite economy measures passenger services ceased quite early at Wooler, on and from 22 September 1930, having run for only 43 years. Freight continued, with the Second World War bringing a temporary increase, but the severe floods of 1948 cut the line between Wooler and Ilderton to the south; this section was never repaired and instead the line was run as two separate branches. The section from Ilderton to Alnwick closed completely in March 1953, and that from Wooler to Coldstream in March 1965.

Above: The 1963 'Scottish Rambler' tour on 14 April has arrived back at Coldstream from Wooler, lightweight Ivatt 2-6-0 No 46474 used on that branch being at the rear of the train. 'B1' No 61324, which has worked up light engine after turning at Tweedmouth shed, will now take the special westwards through Kelso to Roxburgh. Coldstream station is actually in Cornhill-on-Tweed, and was originally called Cornhill from its opening in 1849 until 1873. Coldstream then had the rare distinction of its station being in one country and the town itself in another, the two being separated by the River Tweed; Hay-on-Wye also shared this peculiarity. The route through Coldstream featured in the longest non-stop runs in British history, of 408.6 miles, when the main line north of Berwick was breached by floods in 1948 and the diverted 'Flying Scotsman' came this way. The previous record was 7.2 miles shorter, and had been set in November 1936 between Euston and Glasgow.

Left: A through railway started at Reston on the East Coast Main Line and ran to Ravenswood Junction on the Waverley Route; the first section to be opened, by the NBR in 1849, was to here at Duns from Reston. The line initially ran by the level fertile region of The Merse, which extends about 20 miles along the north bank of the Tweed and is about 10 miles in breadth. It was 1865 before the Berwickshire Railway, pushing westwards, finally reached the Waverley Route. The line suffered during the severe floods of 1948 and the section west of Duns to Greenlaw was never repaired; instead it was operated as two branch lines from either end. Passenger services from Duns to Reston ceased from 10 September 1951, with freight carrying on until 7 November 1966. It will be about another 3½ years before this final closure as 'B1' No 61324 stands at Duns with the 'Scottish Rambler No 2' joint SLS/BLS Easter rail tour of 1963.

Above: A 'Deltic'-hauled Anglo-Scottish express races south through Burnmouth in July 1963. Burnmouth had been the junction station for the short branch to Eyemouth, which opened in 1891 but was closed from 5 February 1962; the track has already been lifted from the branch bay on the right, and also from the goods yard on the left. The fleet of 22 'Deltics' entered service during 1961-62, replacing 55 steam locomotives. They were the most powerful diesels on BR at the time, and when the prototype was built in 1955 it was the most powerful individual diesel locomotive in the world. This unidentified and unnamed 'Deltic' is still in two-tone green, but has had a yellow warning panel applied to its nose. Because of their high cost of manufacture, the locomotives were very intensively used on the fastest high-mileage diagrams, and D9010 was the first class member to achieve two million miles, doing so in January 1973 in just under 12 years of revenue-earning service. *A. Maund*

Left: An unidentified English Electric Type 4 rounds the curve northbound on a coal train at Burnmouth, again in July 1963. Two hundred of the class were built and this appears to be one of the last series, from D345 to D399, which were built with a solid four-character route box on the locomotive's nose. The passenger service through Burnmouth station, which closed from 5 February 1962, had featured in a House of Commons speech by Minister of Transport Ernest Marples. From 23 to 29 October 1960 the Scottish Region had carried out a costing survey that listed train services showing the worst deficits. The most notorious of all the services listed, and that with which Mr Marples made play while discussing the Transport Bill, was the 7.48pm train from Berwick to Edinburgh. During the days of the survey the total number of passengers varied between just two and eight, giving a receipts figure of a meagre 10 shillings (50p); the movement costs were £164, making it the worst receipts/costs ratio throughout the entire Scottish Region. *A. Maund*

Right: On the SLS/BLS Easter tour of 14 April 1963, 'B1' No 61324 handed over at Hawick to 'A3' 4-6-2 No 60041 *Salmon Trout* for the run to Carlisle. During the First World War, locomotive designer Nigel Gresley saw that the heavy wartime loads were more than the 4-4-2 Atlantic locomotives of the period could handle on their own up the grades from King's Cross to Potters Bar. The wide fireboxes of the 4-4-2s could efficiently burn lots of coal, but the problem was lack of adhesion; the 4-6-2 or Pacific wheel arrangement seemed the solution to heavier expresses in the post-war world. The first locomotive of this new design appeared in 1922 and the class was gradually improved over the years, with *Salmon Trout* entering service in 1934. No 60041's strange name derives from the fact that many of the East Coast Main Line locomotives were named after racehorses, in this case the winner of the 1924 St Leger; *Salmon Trout* was the penultimate member of the class to be withdrawn, in December 1965.

Right: As tour participants throng around 'A4' No 60007 *Sir Nigel Gresley* at Hawick, they have just been witness to one of the highest sustained power outputs ever achieved by the class. No 60007 had taken over the 'Scottish Lowlander' tour of 26 September 1964 at Carlisle, but things did not go according to plan. First, the train had been wrongly announced at Carlisle as a regular service train from Manchester to Glasgow, so 'normal' passengers ended up on it. Second and more important, but probably linked to the above, the train was sent the wrong way on leaving Carlisle; it started along the Caledonian route to Glasgow instead of the North British line to Edinburgh, so had to reverse. All this conspired to make the special late, and gave the opportunity for Driver Maclaren and Fireman Whiteman (both passed firemen) to see what they could do. The ascent to Whitrope Summit involved about 9½ miles at a gradient of 1 in 75-80 with severe curvature near Riccarton. Speed settled down at 36mph on the 1 in 75 and reduced to 33mph on the curves, before accelerating back up to 38mph at the summit; this involved a sustained output of around 2,000edbhp, and much shovelling of coal!

Left: Looking west at Roxburgh (although the station seat says Roxburgh Junction) towards St Boswells and the Waverley Route in April 1963, and 'B1' No 61324 has just arrived on the (by this time) single-track line from Kelso and is running round its train before taking the branch on the left to Jedburgh. Roxburgh station opened with the line in 1850 and looks very well kept; in 1963 it still had the benefit of a passenger service along the Tweed Valley line from St Boswells; there was a total of seven trains daily except Sundays, though only four ran the full length of the route on from Kelso to Tweedmouth and, following reversal, Berwick-upon-Tweed. Passenger services on the line ran for the last time on Saturday 13 June 1964, the final train comprising three coaches pulled by Hawick-based BR Standard Class 2 2-6-0 No 78048. Freight traffic carried on along the St Boswells to Kelso section until that too ceased on and from 1 April 1968.

Left: The powers obtained in 1846 by the NBR for the Kelso branch also authorised the company to build a line from Roxburgh to here at Jedburgh, but these powers were allowed to lapse even though the Kelso branch was built. In May 1855 the Jedburgh Railway Company, for which Thomas Bouch of Tay Bridge fame made surveys and plans, obtained an Act of Parliament to build the line, and it was opened on 17 July 1856. Worked from the beginning by the NBR, it was absorbed by that company in 1860. The July 1922 'Bradshaw' shows six passenger trains in each direction along the seven-mile railway to Roxburgh. Due to flood damage both the passenger and freight services ceased on and from 13 August 1948; following repairs the line was reopened to freight only on 26 August. No 61324 stands at Jedburgh with its enthusiasts' special on 14 April 1963. The station closed completely in 1966 and the area is now an industrial estate.

Above: As mentioned earlier in the book, at Duns, after the through railway between the East Coast Main Line at Reston and the Waverley Route was breached by floods in 1948 the section west of Duns to Greenlaw was never repaired, and the line was instead operated as two separate branches. This is Greenlaw, which both lost its passenger service and became the terminus of the line from Ravenswood Junction on the Waverley Route on and from 13 August 1948, the last trains running through to Duns the day before. Greenlaw has more than once been the county town of Berwickshire, and a cause of much rivalry between it and Duns, the honour changing hands over the centuries; currently it resides with Duns, and has done so since an Act of Parliament in 1903. 'B1' No 61324 is running round the 'Scottish Rambler No 2' joint SLS/BLS Easter rail tour on 14 April 1963. Freight ceased in 1965 and the station building is now a private residence.

Left: 'A4' No 60031 *Golden Plover* is at speed on the Waverley Route passing Bowland, a few miles north of Galashiels; the name of the route was derived from the novel by Sir Walter Scott. It is Sunday 18 April 1965, and *Golden Plover* is hauling the 'Scottish Rambler No 4' tour from Glasgow to Edinburgh and Carlisle, then back to Glasgow; approximately 250 miles with the one locomotive. Just visible is the yellow diagonal stripe on the cab side, which indicates that No 60031 was not allowed on the electrified main line south of Crewe after 1 September 1964. Double-tracked throughout, this route saw much heavy freight traffic, especially once the marshalling yards at Kingmoor, Carlisle and Millerhill, Edinburgh, were open. Despite many protests, the Waverley Route was shut at the beginning of 1969, the last passenger train being the Edinburgh to London St Pancras through sleeper service. But trains will soon run again through Bowland: the Scottish Parliament passed the Waverley Railway (Scotland) Act in June 2006 for the line to be rebuilt from Newcraighall, Edinburgh, to Tweedbank, Galashiels.

Right: At Niddrie West Junction, Edinburgh, we have a close-up of the corridor tender paired with 'A4' No 60009 *Union of South Africa* as it prepares to couple up to the 'Scottish Lowlander' tour of 26 September 1964. The 'Flying Scotsman' non-stop service commenced on 1 May 1928 between King's Cross and Edinburgh, a distance of about 400 miles. To allow this to be performed without undue strain on the engine crew, Nigel Gresley designed and patented his corridor tender, which enabled a spare crew to travel in the front compartment of the train and be able to relieve the first crew half-way. Ten of these tenders were built, and incorporated a corridor 18 inches wide by 5 feet high along the right-hand side when viewed from the rear; there was a circular window at the back for illumination. These 10 plus 11 more new-build tenders were fitted to the 'A4' class in the 1930s, as they had taken over the long non-stop runs from the original 'A1s' and 'A3s'; non-corridor tenders were also used on the 'A4s'.

Above: The North British shed at Edinburgh St Margarets (64A) was situated on the south of the East Coast Main Line, to the east of Waverley station. It was a very cramped location, and during the Second World War the LNER even resorted to out-stationing a number of freight locomotives at Seafield shed, Leith, which belonged to the competing CR/LMS and had been rented out for £200 annually. This panorama was taken on Sunday 5 October 1963 and prominent are three BR Standard Class 4 2-6-4Ts, the one nearest the camera being No 80114, which was at 64A from March 1962 until withdrawal at the end of December 1966. Noticeable on No 80114, relative to the 'J37' next to it, is the pleasing curved profile given to the side tanks and bunker to comply with the BR L1 loading gauge. No 80114 was built at Doncaster and entered service in December 1954; however, on its way north to Polmadie it was temporarily commandeered by York for Scarborough services.

On the same day at St Margarets was 'A1' 4-6-2 No 60151 *Midlothian*. The entire class of 49 was built after nationalisation during 1948/49; No 60151 was one of the 23 built at Darlington, with the rest at Doncaster. The 64 new-construction boilers, shared with the 15 'A2/3s' such as the now preserved *Blue Peter*, used 2% nickel-steel in the barrel plates for a weight saving of 7cwt. Twenty-five more replacement boilers were built, including five as late as 1961. The class had a double blastpipe and Kylchap cowls fitted in a smokebox length designed for a single chimney; as a result there was no space to fit self-cleaning apparatus. They averaged 100,000 miles or more between heavy repairs, with the five examples equipped with roller bearings, which did not included No 60151, averaging 118,000. As most express passenger work had already been dieselised, No 60151 went to Tweedmouth shed (52D) in September 1962 where it was used mainly on freight work; it was withdrawn from York (50A) in November 1965.

Stanier 'Coronation' class No 46251 *City of Nottingham* stands at Edinburgh Princes Street station ready to depart with the return leg of the 'Duchess Commemorative' rail tour on 5 October 1963. Princes Street was the Caledonian Railway terminus in Edinburgh and opened in 1870, replacing the original Lothian Road station. The impressive facility seen here dates from a major rebuilding between 1890 and 1893; it had seven platforms and an 850-foot-long bayed roof, and a hotel was added in 1903. Services were subsequently concentrated on Waverley station, and Princes Street closed in September 1965; it was demolished at the end of the decade, although the hotel still survives as the Caledonian Hilton. The journey back to Crewe had notable spells of sustained high-speed running, more than 77mph for the 36.7 miles from Beattock Summit to Kilpatrick (pass to pass), and what was believed to be an all-time record of 24 minutes and three seconds for the 32.2 miles from Tebay to Lancaster (pass to pass), an average of more than 80mph.

Left and Above: At South Queensferry on 13 April 1963 are No 256 *Glen Douglas* and 'J37' No 64603, top-and-tailing the 'Scottish Rambler' tour. The pair had descended from Dalmeny Junction under the approach arches of the later-constructed famous railway bridge over the Firth of Forth. *Glen Douglas* was a member of the NBR 'K' class, later LNER 'D34', which consisted of 32 locomotives built between 1913 and 1920; they were given the names of Scottish glens, and thus became known as the 'Glen' class. They had superheating from new and in their early years even had pyrometers to measure the steam temperature. Three-quarters of the class were initially allocated to Glasgow Eastfield and were used extensively on the West Highland line, and despite the arrival of newer locomotives they continued to be associated with this steeply graded line until withdrawal, which started in 1946. *Glen Douglas* was withdrawn from regular service in 1959 and restored at Cowlairs Works, Glasgow. It was reported in 1960 that the now preserved 'J36' No 65243 *Maude* worked the South Queensferry branch duty twice daily from Edinburgh, conditionally outwards via Kirkliston (as had No 256) and back via Turnhouse; apparently it had been engaged on this duty ever since it returned from war duties in France after the end of the First World War.

Above: Meanwhile, on the other side of the Forth Estuary at North Queensferry, a six-car DMU bound for Edinburgh climbs the noticeably steep gradient of 1 in 70 up to the bridge, in a view believed to date from 1960. Thomas Bouch proposed a suspension bridge, but following the Tay Bridge disaster this was stopped, despite certain works having started. This internationally recognised Scottish landmark was the first major structure in Britain to be built in steel, more than 50,000 tons being used; the contemporary Eiffel Tower was built of wrought iron. During its construction more than 450 workers were injured and 98 lost their lives. It was opened on 4 March 1890 by the Prince of Wales, who drove home the last rivet. 'Painting the Forth Bridge' is a term used to indicate a never-ending task, but things could be different in the future; the repainting contract, awarded in 2002 and recently completed, used 20,000 square metres of paint and is expected to have a life of at least 25 years. *A. Maund*

2nd - Class
STEPHENSON LOCOMOTIVE SOCIETY
and
BRANCH LINE SOCIETY
13th April 1963,
Edinburgh (Waverley) to
EDINBURGH (WAVERLEY)
via SouthQueensferryKinglassieDollar & Alva
For conditions see over (H
0048

Left: How things have changed today from this evocative panorama looking west at Bathgate. It is believed to date from the summer of 1960, when coal was definitely still king and 'bings' (the Scottish term for waste tips) dominated the horizon. In the foreground is locally allocated 'J35' 0-6-0 No 64510, a member of a non-superheated slide-valve predecessor to the visually similar 'J37' class. Steam did not reign supreme, however, and in the right distance to the left of the locomotive shed can just be seen the yellow and black stripes of a diesel shunter. Passenger services had already ceased in 1956, but optimism was high among local railway staff, as the British Motor Corporation (the merged Austin Motor Company and Morris Motors) truck and tractor plant at Bathgate was due to start production soon and there were hopes that the passenger service might be restored as well. Vehicle production did start in 1961, but the factory closed in 1986, the same year that passenger services were eventually reintroduced from Bathgate to Edinburgh. *A. Maund*

Right: Seen on the same day at Bathgate is 'J36' No 65277, with Edinburgh Road beyond. Devolved government has proved a boon for the Scottish rail system, and Holyrood has set three priorities for its transport policies: promoting sustainable economic growth; improving journey times and connectivity; and improving accessibility and affordability. Following a study in 2002-03, reinstatement of the railway between Bathgate and Airdrie (Drumgelloch), closed to passenger traffic in 1956, was identified as a priority. The work was approved by the Scottish Parliament in May 2006, and the line was officially opened in March 2011. The route is double track and electrified throughout, with a 15-minute service frequency in both directions between Edinburgh Waverley and either Helensburgh or Milngavie via Bathgate, Airdrie and Glasgow Queen Street Low Level. A new depot to service the EMUs has been built at Bathgate on the site of the former STVA new car pound, and Bathgate station has been relocated to become a major park-and-ride centre with the benefit of a 400-space car park. *A. Maund*

Left: These two views taken at Bathgate shed (64F) are thought to date from the summer of 1960. The *Railway Observer* noted 24 locomotives around the shed on 23 August 1960, 13 of which were available for work, including 'J36s' Nos 65341/46 seen in the first photograph, two were under repair, five were stored, and four were dumped near the coal stage. Bathgate was an ex-North British depot, and it was noted that all the dumped locomotives were Caley intruders, Nos 55210, 55229, 57560 and 55165, as seen in the second photograph; all had been allocated to Dalry Road (64C), a CR depot. Bathgate was one of a number of places used by BR to store the ever-growing numbers of surplus steam locomotives in the early 1960s, and on 31 March 1962, 29 locomotives were noted, including powerful main-line examples – 11 'V2s', an 'A3' and an 'A1' – although these last two were stored inside, greased down and under tarpaulins. Of the four dumped CR locos noted above in 1960, all except No 55210 were seen at Thornton on 15 March 1962 being towed by a 'J37' and presumed bound for Inverurie Works for cutting up.
A. Maund

Above: The author only ever visited Bathgate shed (64F) once, on Saturday 16 October 1965, hoping to see *Maude*, the last remaining named 'J36' 0-6-0. Unfortunately the locomotive was not there, but gently simmering away outside the depot was classmate No 65267, adjacent to a BR Standard Class 4 2-6-0. This exceptionally long-lived design had been introduced by the North British Railway as its Class C in 1888, and 168 had been built when production stopped in 1900. They were used all over the NBR network, initially for long-distance goods work. During the First World War, 25 were loaned to the Government for the duration for use in France, and in 1919 these were named after military leaders and places connected with the war. As newer and more powerful locomotives arrived, the 'J36s' were used more on local work, their small size and excellent route availability making them ideal for lightly laid branch lines. Although withdrawals had started in 1926, the last two survived until 1967 to become the final BR steam locomotives in Scotland.

Left: These two photographs were taken during July 1963 at the Bonnybridge Silica & Fireclay Company Ltd. The locomotive is Caledonian Railway 3F 0-6-0 No 57592, a class introduced by McIntosh in 1899; this example was withdrawn in August 1963. The Bonnybridge area is rich in minerals, especially coal and clay; although it never became one of the main coal-mining areas, it was a different matter with the clay. Clay here is not the type you see on a potter's wheel, but a solid hard rock laid down millions of years ago as mud at the bottom of lakes and seas. Over the millennia it has been squeezed hard to form a solid rock that can be crushed by hammers and machines into a very fine powder, which is then mixed with water and can be moulded into bricks. The special clays around Bonnybridge were used to make a whole variety of different bricks and tiles. There were a number of brickworks in the area, the quality of the bricks was very high, and they were used all over the country and even exported. The Bonnybridge Silica & Fireclay Company operated as a manufacturer of bricks and ceramic products, originating as a partnership in 1874; the works closed in 1973. The branch from the works connected with the NBR's Glasgow to Edinburgh main line, a few miles to the west of Falkirk High. *A. Maund*

Right: The track is lost in the undergrowth as No 57592 shunts at the Bonnybridge Silica & Fireclay Company works in July 1963. Before nationalisation only the LNER had dedicated brick-carrying wagons, but they were bogie vehicles with a capacity of 50 tons; instead it was normal to use ordinary open wagons packed with straw. To transport bricks more efficiently some medium goods open wagons were converted in the mid-1950s to 'Palbricks', the strange name being derived from what the wagons were used for, carrying wooden pallets loaded with bricks. Newly constructed wagons in three designs then followed, with different body widths for different pallet sizes. All had plywood side panels with two reinforced slots, allowing them to be lifted out by fork-lift truck, the side stanchions then being removed for loading. In all, 1,420 'Palbricks' were built, but by the late 1960s most were out of use and many were converted for other purposes. Visit www.palbrick.com to follow the restoration of one of these wagons. *A. Maund*

This is the site of Glenboig station, with a train hauled by D5126 approaching from the Stirling direction on Saturday 5 June 1965. The Caledonian Railway had opened a line through here in 1848 as its main route to the north – this was the central 'prong' of Charles Stewart's 'trident' mentioned earlier, with the left and right prongs going to Glasgow and Edinburgh. However, the station didn't open until 1879, and was closed in 1956. The population of Glenboig increased from only 120 in 1860 to 1,500 in 1890, and nearly all the houses formerly belonged to the Glenboig Union Fireclay Company, whose works were said to be the largest of their kind in the world. The reputation of the goods produced at the works was such that medals were awarded from all over the world, including Chile, India and Australia; the works were demolished in 1958. Recently there have been plans to build a giant rail freight terminal between Glenboig and Coatbridge, but they have met with local opposition. *A. Maund*

Right: This time we are looking the other way at Glenboig station, also on 5 June 1965. By the far platform are Garnqueen North Junction signalbox and a very impressive telegraph pole with different types of insulators on it. The tracks on the left head for Garnqueen South Junction, Coatbridge and England, while those on the right are the Hayhill Fork to Gartcosh Junction and Glasgow Buchanan Street. The Hayhill Fork was not built until 17 years after the opening of Buchanan Street, and it was a further four years before passenger services were routed over this section; until then the Caledonian Railway seemed quite happy to use Queen Street station as the terminus for its services from the North. The approaching train is headed by D5132, double-heading with another member of the same class, most probably an Inverness-bound service as at the time a consecutively numbered batch of 19 of these diesels, including D5132, was allocated to Inverness shed (60A). *A. Maund*

Left: In the early 1960s the express passenger work performed by Gresley's 'A4s' along the East Coast Main Line gradually became less and less as more replacement diesels were built: the non-stop 'Elizabethan' ran for the last time in 1961, five of the class were withdrawn at the end of 1962, and King's Cross Top Shed closed in June 1963. This sort of thing was happening all over the BR network as modernisation continued apace. However, an exception was the Glasgow-Aberdeen expresses, from which the locally manufactured Bo-Bo diesels of the D61xx series had been removed and largely retired to less exacting work. Following a trial on the route with No 60027 on 22 February 1962, the remaining 'A4s' were transferred to Scotland; by May 1964 only one was still allocated in England. This photograph was taken near Cumbernauld on 6 June 1965; few would have thought that the final work of the 'A4s' would be over the old Caledonian main line between Aberdeen and Glasgow, and it continued until September 1966. *A. Maund*

Above: It wasn't just BR steam that could be seen in the Glenboig area – this is nearby Bedlay Colliery in May 1978. No 9 was a Hudswell Clarke product of 1909, the oldest locomotive at Bedlay, and it is seen drawing loaded wagons away from the coal screens. There were no facilities for the locomotives here and they were serviced and stored in the open. No 9 was the most popular locomotive at Bedlay and often worked to the exchange sidings with BR about a mile away on the old Monkland & Kirkintilloch Railway; withdrawal came in 1979 after foundation ring problems in the firebox. The colliery had opened in 1905 to produce high-quality coking coal for Gartsherrie Iron Works, and by 1969 almost 1,000 people were employed here producing around 250,000 tons annually. Winding of coal stopped in December 1981, by which time the site had become the last to use conventional steam locomotives on a regular commercial basis in Scotland; it was also the last deep mine in the Monklands.

Left: July 1963 found a row of three Caledonian locomotives at the north end of Stirling shed, which had been recoded 65J from April 1960 and, despite being of Caledonian origin, was under the North British shed at Glasgow Eastfield. No 57252 is a Drummond 'Standard Goods' or 'Jumbo' 0-6-0, introduced in 1883 and withdrawn from Stirling in November 1962. No 54501 was an example of the final class of the famous 'Caley Bogies', and had been withdrawn from Glasgow St Rollox in December 1961. In front of the gasometer is No 57679, representing the final development of CR 0-6-0s, introduced by Pickersgill in 1918. Although more imposing, this modern design was less efficient and a number were withdrawn in the 1930s, but superheating stopped the rot. To No 57679 fell the dubious honour of being the last Caledonian locomotive in service when it was withdrawn, together with eight other CR engines, on 29 November 1963, although it seems that it had not seen use for some time previously. *A. Maund*

Right: As a young lad the author was always intrigued by the name and location of this station – Port of Menteith. Although close by the River Forth, it is some way inland and quite isolated 13 miles west of Stirling where the Forth takes on the appearance of a very meandering rural waterway, the antithesis of where you would think a port ought to be. The actual village of Port of Menteith is on the Lake (not Loch) of Menteith, some miles to the north, and when the Forth & Clyde Junction Railway was opened through here in 1856 the station was originally called Cardross, the name being changed in 1858. This country line was operated by the North British and a number of the stations were some way from the places they purported to serve. Not surprisingly passenger services ceased quite early on, in 1934, but freight continued from the Stirling end to here until October 1959; this view looking east dates from 1960. The July 1961 *Railway Magazine* reported that the British Transport Commission was inviting offers for the rental of Port of Menteith station and others along the F&CJR as caravan sites. *A. Maund*

The original transparency carries no identification at all, and neither do the three other photos taken at the same location on the same day, although from the type of film used the date is about 1960. Initially the author thought the locomotive was 'J37' No 64618 from Thornton Junction (62A), but on closer examination it seemed that No 64613 from St Margarets (64A) was more likely. Other clues were that the level crossing seems to have had double track at some time, none of the houses look to have TV aerials, so presumably this area may be shielded from the Central Valley, the hills in the background look quite high and distinctive, and the row of houses must surely still exist today. Despite days of research, copious use of Google Earth and suggestions from fellow enthusiasts, the answer eventually came following a Festiniog Railway Society film show by the author – it is Rowantree Terrace, Lennoxtown, and the row of houses has been demolished for some years. *A. Maund*

Left: The railway to Lennoxtown, with the Campsie Fells in the background, was opened as early as 1848 from Lenzie. Starting in 1866 an extension was opened from Blane Valley Junction at Lennoxtown, reaching the Forth & Clyde Railway and eventually Aberfoyle, the original station at Lennoxtown becoming goods-only. A through Glasgow to Aberfoyle passenger service operated this way, and in 1951 three trains covered the full distance, with a further four running as far as Lennoxtown; however, all passenger services ceased in September of that year. 'J37' No 64613 is just south of Lennoxtown and is standing on the bridge over the Glazert Water, having just crossed the B822; evidence of the second track that once existed up to Blane Valley Junction can be seen in the dimensions of the bridge. By this time the line was freight-only to Campsie Glen, where it served the Lennox Castle Mental Hospital, which had its own railway siding; complete closure at Lennoxtown came in 1966. *A. Maund*

Right: Glasgow Queen Street High Level station is extremely cramped and hemmed in by a tunnel to the north and the city to the south. A much smaller station than Glasgow Central, it is nevertheless today the third busiest in Scotland, with nearly five million passengers annually. The gradient in the tunnel at the end of the platforms is a fearsome 1 in 42, and trains were once hauled up it by rope. At the time of this 1960 photograph the nearby Buchanan Street station was still open; however, with the active dislike in the Beeching era of duplicate facilities, this was closed in 1966 and services were concentrated here. The short length of the platforms can create problems, and when Inter-City 125 HSTs called they had to use Platform 7, with the end of the train close to the tunnel mouth. Future thoughts involve electrification and, while keeping the number of platforms the same, to make more of them capable of accepting six-car trains. *A. Maund*

Left and below left: A rare, and unique in the author's experience, double-heading combination was a 'Clan' and a 'Britannia', but this is the combination at the head of the 'Thames-Clyde Express' ready to leave the long-closed G&SWR terminus of Glasgow St Enoch on Monday 11 May 1959, the day the author's father returned home to Worcestershire. He left East Kilbride on the 8.05am bus to Glasgow at a cost of 1s 1d, then got the Underground from Buchanan Street to St Enoch for 2d. The plan was to cause some confusion by presenting himself at St Enoch and ask for a ticket to Worcester via Kilmarnock, Leeds and Sheffield on the 'Thames-Clyde Express', instead of using the more obvious route from Glasgow Central via Beattock and Crewe. However, it caused absolutely no confusion at all with the Booking Office staff, and a ticket was promptly issued, although the cost, at £2 19s 4d via Sheffield, was 5s 8d more than via Crewe. No 70054 *Dornoch Firth* was the last 'Britannia' built, and is coupled to one of the larger BR1D tenders fitted to the final ten members of the class; these had a larger capacity of 9 tons of coal, with a steam-powered coal pusher, and 4,725 gallons of water. No 70054 departed from St Enoch on time at 9.20am and worked through to Leeds City, arriving late at 2.26pm due to signals outside the station; it was allocated to Leeds Holbeck (55A) at the time. 'Clan' No 72005 *Clan Macgregor* had a home depot of Carlisle Kingmoor (12A) in May 1959, and piloted the 'Thames-Clyde Express' all the way to a 12.05pm arrival at Carlisle. At Leeds 'Black Five' No 44919 took over and, following changes of train at Sheffield Midland and Birmingham New Street, arrival at Worcester Shrub Hill was at 7.37pm.

Right: Standing ready at Glasgow Central in April 1963 is 'Royal Scot' class No 46156 *The South Wales Borderer*, heading a relief to the 'Royal Scot' train. The locomotive is a very long way from its home depot of Holyhead (6J), although it was transferred to Willesden (1A) in June 1963. The whole class was rebuilt starting in 1942 and finishing in 1955, and it was considered a great success, with the rebuilt engines standing up to high-speed running, heavy loads and wartime neglect better than the originals; in the 1948 locomotive trials the class performed particularly well. Glasgow Central was opened by the Caledonian Railway on 31 July 1879, and rebuilt between 1901 and 1905. The overhead power lines visible here first appeared for the Cathcart Circle Line electrification, which started on 28 May 1962; the voltage is 6.25kV instead of the usual 25kV, and was used at this time where there were reduced clearances for the overhead cable. Today Glasgow Central is the busiest station in the UK outside London.

Right: The epic performance of *Sir Nigel Gresley* over the Waverley Route hauling the 'Scottish Lowlander' tour of 26 September 1964 has already been mentioned, and a consequence of such high power levels was that the amount of coal remaining in the tender of No 60007 became a concern. *Union of South Africa* was the reserve for the tour, and was called on to take it over at Edinburgh; No 60009 is seen at Glasgow St John's, where it had to detach from the train to take water. At this time the locomotive's usual work was on the 3-hour expresses between Glasgow and Aberdeen, the 61B shed plate for Aberdeen Ferryhill being prominent on the streamlined front end. No 60009 was the last engine to receive a general repair by its makers, just before Doncaster Works finished with steam in November 1963. Above the centre coupled wheel is a rectangular stainless steel plate depicting a springbok, donated by a Bloemfontein newspaper proprietor and fitted on 20 April 1954.

Left: Alan Maund's Worcestershire-plate Ford Consul II looks in tip-top condition as it is passed by a Glasgow tram in this photograph, thought to have been taken in 1960. The Glasgow Corporation Tramways system used to be one of the largest of its kind in Europe, with more than 1,000 trams over the years. The first horse-drawn route was laid in 1872 and electricity was tried experimentally in 1898; it was considered a success, and the horses finished in 1902. The gauge was highly unusual at 4ft 7¾in, which permitted standard-gauge railway wagons to work on the system, their wheel flanges running in the tram track slots. The car appears to be No 1378, which was built in 1951 by Glasgow Corporation Transport. The tram system was gradually closed down, with the final trams operating on 4 September 1962. Apart from Blackpool, the Glasgow system was the last in the UK until the opening of Manchester Metrolink in 1992. *A. Maund*

Left: To the author and his school friends as 11-year-old trainspotters from Worcestershire, the 'Clans' had something of a mythical status, with nobody ever having seen one. During the Easter 1963 visit it was discovered that the five 'Clans' withdrawn from Glasgow Polmadie (66A) during the December 1962 holocaust were still there, out of use. No 72000 was discovered by the shed entrance, but the other four were stored outside in a row. This is No 72002 with its *Clan Campbell* name plate missing, sacking over its chimney and classmates on either side. Very noticeable is the flexible screening between the rear of the cab and front of the tender, a modification fitted in an attempt to reduce cab draughts. The authorities seemed to have been a bit over-enthusiastic with certain of the December 1962 withdrawals, as some were reinstated later, including No 48773, which saw out the end of BR main-line steam in August 1968, but not the five 'Clans', which were cut up at Darlington Works.

Right: Excluding narrow gauge, most people are probably only aware of Brunel's broad gauge in addition to the normal standard gauge in Britain of 4ft 8½in, but in the early 19th century, and mainly around Lanarkshire, a number of railways used the Scotch gauge of 4ft 6in. The Paisley & Renfrew Railway was one of these; it had been authorised in 1835 and opened in 1837 with locomotive haulage from the start. Starting from a wharf on the Clyde, it was 3 miles long and virtually level, but in order to save on costs it changed over to horse haulage in 1842. The original terminus at Paisley Hamilton Street was closed to passengers in 1866 when the line, purchased by the G&SWR in 1852, was converted to standard gauge and connected to the national network. This is the replacement station of Paisley Abercorn on Easter Saturday 1965, as an enthusiasts' special passes through; at this time just one passenger train a day stopped here, and that in one direction only! This sparse unbalanced service also had the distinction of being steam-hauled right to the end of Scottish-based BR steam, with No 80004 hauling the service on Friday 28 April 1967.

Left: The River Clyde at Erskine was shallow enough to cross on foot until the 18th century, when it was deepened to allow large ships to sail to Glasgow. The ferry crossing used to be maintained by Lord Blantyre, but the Clyde Navigation Trust acquired the Erskine Ferry in the early 20th century and added a vehicle ferry boat to the old passenger service from Erskine (in Renfrewshire) to Old Kilpatrick (in West Dunbartonshire). This view of the Erskine Ferry dates from 1959; it is a chain ferry, meaning that it is guided across the River Clyde by chains connected to both shores. In the early 1960s questions were asked in Parliament about a replacement high-level bridge, and a traffic census report was compiled. The ferry service closed down in 1971 when the newly built Erskine Bridge opened. The ramped jetties survive on both sides of the River Clyde, with the new bridge slightly downstream (to the left).

Right: The Forth & Clyde Junction Railway was a mostly rural line connecting settlements in the Forth Valley from Stirling to Loch Lomond and the River Leven. Constituted in 1853, it was worked by the NBR, which leased the line in 1875, but it retained its independent constitution with its own directors and secretary until the Railways Act of 1921 caused incorporation into the LNER. This is the signalbox at Jamestown, three-quarters of a mile from Balloch, in 1959. In 1922 there were five passenger trains each way, four of which worked over the entire length from Balloch to Stirling. The line was popular in summer as part of the 'Trossachs Tour': by rail over the Forth & Clyde to Aberfoyle, coach to Loch Katrine, steamer to Stronachlachar, coach to Inversnaid on Loch Lomond, then steamer to Balloch. Passenger services here finished from 1 October 1934, and freight east of Jamestown ceased in October 1959; however, the goods service from the west over the River Leven continued until September 1964.

Left: One of the very distinctive electric 'Blue Trains' calls at Craigendoran with a Helensburgh Central to Airdrie service on 3 June 1965, its livery recalling that used for locomotives of the former Caledonian Railway. At this time there were trains every half an hour over the full 35 miles, but far more over the central tunnel section through Glasgow Queen Street Low Level. However, their introduction had been a different matter and involved one of the most outstanding acts of prompt organisation by any British railway. When the electric service commenced on 7 November 1960 the steam locomotives previously used were transferred away, depots were closed and there was considerable rearrangement of staff and facilities. But following a series of transformer explosions, the decision was made to withdraw the entire fleet of 72 electric sets in the middle of the night at 1.38am on Sunday 18 December 1960; by the Monday morning a steam service had been reintroduced with only a few hitches. A detailed description of the emergency restoration of the Clydeside steam suburban services appeared in the July 1961 *Trains Illustrated. A. Maund*

Right: The electrified route to Helensburgh can be seen lower down to the left in this view of D8072 coming off the West Highland line with a short freight, taken on the same day as the previous 'Blue Train' photograph; the two routes joined at Craigendoran Junction. In their early days referred to as 'English Electric Type 1s', these locomotives are now generally called Class 20s, and were the first to be delivered from the pilot scheme that was supposed to allow BR to gain experience of diesel operation before standardising types for mass-production. However, events overtook the pilot scheme, with a national recession causing BR to try and halt the financial downturn by accelerating the replacement of steam by diesel. Large diesel orders were placed, in some cases before a single prototype had taken to the rails, and a motley collection of designs were built – some good, some bad and some indifferent. However, these 'English Electric Type 1s' proved to be an immediate success and 228 were eventually built. *A. Maund*

Right: It is difficult to remember after so many years whether it was the author or his father who took particular photographs. There isn't much doubt with this one, though, at Greenock Princes Pier on 17 April 1965, with HR No 103 arriving over rusty tracks on a 'Scottish Rambler' rail tour, as the author's father is at bottom left using a cine camera; the scheduled arrival time was 4.47pm. It was announced the following month that all four of the Scottish Region preserved locomotives, including HR103, were to be withdrawn from active service and placed in the Glasgow Museum of Transport. This large terminal on the quayside at Greenock was opened in 1869, originally some 90 yards to the right and initially called Greenock Albert Harbour. It saw both tourists and commuters for the Clyde steamers, as well as 'Cunarder' boat trains connecting with the Cunard Canadian services, a direct Glasgow service that continued after withdrawal of the regular passenger service on 2 February 1959. No 80046 was seen on the first 'Cunarder' of 1960 on 14 January, running from St Enoch and preceded by a dedicated parcels train with No 42741; these services carried on until 30 November 1965.

Right: Of all the various dumps the author and his father visited, this one at Carnbroe, near Airdrie, in April 1962 always seemed to be visually especially memorable. The writer of the report about it in the May 1962 *Railway Observer* clearly thought the same: 'The collection of withdrawn engines at Carnbrae (sic) presents a particularly macabre sight. Almost all have the tall Caley (principally stovepipe) chimneys, and in combination with their low empty tenders are oddly reminiscent of views of Swindon yard at the time of conversion from the Broad Gauge. Stored with the engines are a number of bolster wagons, while copious vegetation and young trees recently cut back will grow again strongly and make the scene, if left undisturbed, even more fantastic.' Many of the locomotives here were from Polmadie and Motherwell; on 3 March there were 34 present, and 29 by 9 June. The dump was well located as there were many private contractors who cut up scrap locomotives in the Airdrie, Coatbridge and Motherwell areas.

Right: The combined effects of steam being replaced following the 1955 Modernisation Plan, together with a general contraction of business being done by the railways, resulted in masses of surplus steam locomotives, not just in Scotland but all over the UK. Previously the railway's own workshops would generally cut up withdrawn locomotives, but by the early 1960s there were so many of them that private contractors were used, and it became a common sight to see rows of scrapped steam locomotives awaiting their fate. Here are two further views of the dump at Carnbroe Sidings during Easter 1962; the sidings were then the terminus of the former North British Coatbridge to Bothwell branch, and the houses with the red roofs in the background are in Elgin Place. No 55267 is another of the same class of ten 0-4-4Ts as seen withdrawn at Carstairs, although this one has a stovepipe chimney and was withdrawn from Greenock (Ladyburn) in October 1961, the same month that 0-6-0T No 56298 was withdrawn from Polmadie.

Left: In May 1978 the author's father paid a visit to R. B. Tennent's foundry at Whifflet, Coatbridge. Established in 1857, the foundry quickly grew to become the largest roll-making unit in Britain; at its height it produced 40% of the chilled cast-iron rolls and 60% of the cast-steel rolls manufactured in the UK, and the steel rolls were the largest made in the country. *Denis* is a vertical-boilered and chain-driven Sentinel locomotive. The Sentinel company began as Alley & MacLellan, based in Polmadie, Glasgow, in 1906, moving to Shrewsbury in 1915. After financial problems it was reorganised as the Sentinel Waggon Works (1920) Ltd, and led the market for steam-powered road vehicles in the 1920s and '30s, using the technology to also produce steam shunting locomotives. Tennent's eventually had four of this type of locomotive, and *Denis* was the final development of the 'BE' type. They were the final commercially operated steam locomotives in Scotland and lasted until 1984.

Right: Caledonian Railway No 123 was built at the Hyde Park Works of Neilson & Co in Springburn, Glasgow, during 1886, in just 66 days, for the Edinburgh Exhibition held that year, where it won a gold medal. It was the only member of its class, and achieved fame in the 1888 'Race to the North' between Carlisle and Edinburgh by covering the 100¾ miles in 102½ minutes with a four-coach train. Soon superseded by more powerful types, regular jobs became hauling the directors' saloon and pilot to the Royal Train. No 123 was withdrawn in 1935, when it was the last working single-wheeler; it was kept in impeccable condition at St Rollox Works until 1957, then, inspired by the success of the restoration of GWR *City of Truro* to working order, the same was done to No 123. Immaculate as always, the locomotive stands at Cleland on 19 April 1965 with the BLS 'Scottish Rambler No 4' rail tour, coupled to two restored CR coaches.

Left: Motherwell shed (66B) lay in the centre of an iron-making and coal-mining district, and was plagued by ground settlement from long-forgotten underground workings, while above ground 'bings' (waste tips) loomed. During the Second World War a simplified version of the LMS Stanier 2-8-0 was called for by the Ministry of Supply, and the resulting War Department locomotive was made using 20% fewer man hours, together with fewer steel castings and forgings. This 2-10-0 version was further developed from the 2-8-0 to get the axleload down to 13½ tons and to favour combustion of low-grade coals by using a wide firebox with 40sq ft of grate above the frames, in comparison with the 28.6sq ft narrow grate inside the frames of the 2-8-0. After the war BR ended up with 733 of the 2-8-0s, but only 25 of the 2-10-0s, which had the better steam-raising and running characteristics. 'WD' 2-10-0 No 90761 is seen at its home depot of Motherwell during Easter 1962; it was withdrawn in November of that year.

Left: These compact, chunky and distinctive short-wheelbase 0-6-0Ts were intended for use in dockyards and depots where track curvature was likely to be severe and loads heavy. The ten class members were built at Derby during 1928/29, and when new went to Scotland, Merseyside and Fleetwood. They were in some ways slightly reminiscent of the numerous 'Jinty' 0-6-0s, and although designed at Horwich they had a Derby feel to them. The rear coupled axlebox was carried in Cartazzi slides and the coupling rods had ball joints, both for increased flexibility, and as a result of this, together with the short 9ft 6in wheelbase, they could negotiate a curve of 2 chains radius. Although the number is not visible, in the background above the boiler of the 'Black Five' is a second member of the class, No 47168. Both Nos 47163 and 47168 came here to Hamilton shed (66C) during the five-week period ended 10 March 1962 from Greenock (Ladyburn) (66D), a month before this photograph was taken.

Left: Hamilton shed was some yards to the north of Hamilton West station, and is seen here during an Easter 1962 visit. The ten-road shed suffered from subsidence problems from old coal workings in the same way as nearby Motherwell; dating from the 1880s, it had this brick-built coaling stage with a water tank on top of it. The locomotive is Motherwell-allocated CR standard shunting tank No 56336, a member of the '782' class, of which 138 were built between 1898 and 1922. No 56336 ended up as one of the final three still in service, all being withdrawn at the end of 1962. The three pioneering Leyland diesel railcars, built in 1933 and withdrawn in 1951, also operated from Hamilton shed, and in 1947 the allocation was made up of 53 locomotives together with the railcars. On 6 July 1959 diesel railcars again began to operate from here, and by 1960 four shed roads were given over for their maintenance.

Right: Also on Hamilton shed (66C) by the turntable on the same day are two locomotives that appear to be stored and out of use. At the rear is Fairburn 2-6-4T No 42164, which had been a Hamilton locomotive for years and was formally withdrawn in the mass slaughter of Scottish Region locomotives at the end of 1962. In front is 'J72' No 68733, one of a number of this class that spent time at Hamilton, arriving in October 1961 and being withdrawn in the six weeks ended 18 August 1962; it was cut up at Connell & Co's Calder scrapyard, Coatbridge. Although introduced in 1898 by William Worsdell, the 'J72s' were built at various times over a span of 53 years by the NER, LNER and BR – 113 locomotives in nine batches up to 1951 – a unique record. We have already seen one of the celebrity class members at Newcastle, but they also ended up a long way from their NER origins – Keith and Aberdeen in the north, and even Wrexham in Wales.

The Caledonian Railway line to Hamilton had opened in 1849 and tapped the many coal mines in the area. The North British did not arrive with its railway, seen here, until 1877, and was regarded at the time as an invasion of Caley territory in Lanarkshire, this being the last attack. The first photograph shows Bothwell station, looking north in May 1959, and the second is a close-up of the by then boarded-up signalbox. A little further north was Bothwell Junction, giving direct routes for the coal traffic to both Parkhead Forge via Shettleston Junction and the ironworks at Coatbridge. The Glasgow, Bothwell, Hamilton & Coatbridge Railway was authorised to build these two lines, which connected with the existing NBR Edinburgh to Glasgow via Bathgate route, and it amalgamated retrospectively with the NBR in 1878. Because of the First World War, Bothwell station and others locally were closed from 1 January 1917 until 2 June 1919, and after the Grouping the line was referred to as the LNER Hamilton branch. The passenger service on the branch was substantial; in 1930, 17 trains came via Shettleston Junction and eight via Coatbridge, the latter worked by Sentinel railcar No 37 *Clydesdale*. The future of the Shettleston line seemed assured in 1951 when both construction of a new station was announced, serving Calderpark Zoo, and the line was recommended for electrification in the Inglis Report on passenger transport around Glasgow. However, the Coatbridge line passenger service succumbed in September 1951. The following year saw a complete reversal of thoughts as mining subsidence occurred once more, this time affecting Craighead Viaduct, just south of Bothwell, and the last trains ran through to Hamilton on 13 September 1952. The now truncated branch did not survive long, and closure of the remaining passenger services took effect on and from 4 July 1955; freight carried on until 1961, mainly in the form of a daily working to Bothwell Gas Works.

Left: Thorntonhall, on the East Kilbride branch from Busby, opened with the line to all traffic on 1 September 1868, although a mineral-only service had worked as far east as this from July 1867. The station changed its name from the original Eaglesham Road to Thorntonhall on 1 June 1877, and until LMS days there was a small loop opposite the platform. The line ran through pleasant farming land on the Cathkin Braes and attained a height of 504 feet, involving gradients as steep as 1 in 72. Between Thorntonhall and Hairmyres there used to be three mine or quarry branches. Passenger services originally ran to Glasgow South Side (Gushetfaulds) until 1 July 1879, when they transferred to Bridge Street, being extended to Central on its opening a month later. By 1900 the branch weekday passenger service was about a dozen trains, and this had nearly doubled by 1939. From 31 August 1959 all services transferred to St Enoch, but following that station's closure in 1966 they again terminated at Central.

Right: At the time of this 1959 view, East Kilbride was the terminus for passenger workings from Glasgow. The line opened in 1868, and an extension was built in 1883 to Hamilton, but had a short life; the scant shuttle passenger service that began in 1888 was withdrawn on 1 October 1914 and the track lifted. However, it was relaid in 1919 and one train each way was reintroduced between 1 October 1923 and 14 July 1924. The coal trains from Hamilton to Ardrossan did not pass over the extension, and with little traffic of its own it closed to all traffic except for a short section from East Kilbride for local industry. The line from Glasgow was originally included in the south-side electrification scheme, but a closure announcement was made, to take effect from 5 October 1964. The Glasgow & East Kilbride Railway Development Association successfully fought this, and today the station has a half-hourly service to Glasgow, but not with the gas lighting seen here 50 years ago.

Left: Looking extremely overgrown and derelict in the summer of 1958 is the strangely named station of Quarter, the name apparently coming from an old division of a duke's estate. Coal was first extracted at Quarter in the early 1800s and, following the discovery of ironstone in 1854, an iron works was established. At that time there were also a brick and tile works and a lime works. All this led to the construction of the Hamilton & Strathaven Railway, which opened as far as Quarter for goods only on 9 August 1860; passenger services had to wait until 2 February 1863. Originally the station name was Quarter Road, but this was changed to just Quarter on 1 July 1909. A serious derailment occurred nearby on 30 December 1899, killing three and injuring 13. Passenger services came to an end on and from 1 October 1945, but freight lasted until 21 September 1953, and the track was removed the year after this photograph.

Left: This view of High Blantyre, 4¼ miles north-west of Quarter on the Hamilton & Strathaven Railway, was taken from the station footbridge during May 1959. The railway was authorised in 1857 from Strathaven Junction, 60 chains north of the then Hamilton Terminus (later Hamilton West), and followed a circuitous route to Meikle Earnock, then making for Strathaven. The Caledonian Railway worked it from the outset and the line became vested in that company in 1864. The line was singled south of Quarter, but the line north through High Blantyre remained double because of the traffic from local coal mines and Quarter Iron Works. In 1922 there were between eight and ten passenger trains daily each way through High Blantyre, some running direct to and from Glasgow Central via the curve between Auchenraith and Blantyre Junctions. After closure of the rest of the line to Strathaven, the section east from High Blantyre to Strathaven Junction stayed open as a single track for freight only until 1 June 1960.

The first railway to arrive at the market town of Strathaven was the Hamilton & Strathaven via Quarter, which opened throughout for goods and passenger traffic on 2 February 1863. The next development came with the Mid-Lanark lines, authorised by Caledonian Railway Acts of 1896 and 1897, designed to stop penetration of the area by the G&SWR from Darvel. The existing CR line at nearby Stonehouse and Cot Castle was extended west to Strathaven Central and onwards to Darvel via an end-on junction with the G&SWR at County Boundary, opening throughout in 1905. The original H&SR station at Strathaven was to the north of the town and a connecting link was opened in 1904 to the new Central station; both this line and that from Stonehouse approached Strathaven Central from the east over independent viaducts that crossed a tributary of the Avon Water. In this 1959 view only the foreground viaduct from Stonehouse, on a rising gradient of 1 in 66, was still in use; it closed in 1965.

These two photographs were taken at Lugton during the summer of 1958. Lugton was the junction for the 5-mile branch to Beith Town, which had a service of eight trains each way daily except Sundays, one of which was a through train to and from Glasgow St Enoch. On this day the service is in the hands of CR 'Standard Passenger' class 0-4-4T No 55203, complete with stovepipe chimney; it had been allocated to Hurlford (67B) since the 1940s. Prior to 1873 the Glasgow & South Western Railway operated its trains to Kilmarnock via Paisley and Dalry; the more direct route through Lugton was a joint scheme between the G&SWR and CR, with each company appointing four directors. Both the final link of the direct route from Stewarton to Kilmarnock and the Beith branch opened on the same day, 26 June 1873. Passenger services on the Beith Town branch came to an end in November 1962, with freight ceasing in 1964; passenger services on the main line finished at Lugton in 1966, with the last trains calling on Saturday 5 November. Lugton features in another of the Scottish Government's railway investment initiatives. In the 1970s the section between Barrhead and Kilmarnock, almost 17 miles long, was singled with a passing loop left at Lugton. Kilmarnock is broadly comparable in size to Ayr and the same sort of distance from Glasgow, but the rail service is much poorer. A section of double track more than 5 miles long, referred to as a 'dynamic loop', and costing some £26 million, has been put back between Lugton and Stewarton; the work also involved building second platforms at the single-platform stations of Dunlop and Stewarton. This will permit the Kilmarnock-Glasgow passenger service to be doubled in frequency to half-hourly, matching the service level that Ayr already enjoys.

Left: One of the things for which Dr Beeching became famous in the 1960s was his dislike of duplicate routes between places, and the same was evident some 30 years earlier. This is Auchenmade station in 1958, looking north. The Lanarkshire & Ayrshire Railway through Auchenmade was built to provide a service from Ardrossan to Glasgow, and the line was operated by the Caledonian Railway, opening in September 1888. This new railway was in competition with the Glasgow & South Western Railway, which already had a railway open for nearly 50 years between the same places. This resulted in fierce rivalry, with the CR opening an extension in 1903 to avoid revenue-sharing with the G&SWR. In the 1923 Grouping of railway companies, both the CR and G&SWR ended up together in the new London, Midland & Scottish Railway. Now just one company was providing duplicate services and the inevitable happened – the passenger service through Auchenmade ceased in 1932, the line closing completely in 1953.

Right: The author's father travelled to Carstairs from Wolverhampton High Level on 8 May 1959, arriving there at 3.18pm. He then caught the 3.32pm service to Lanark on his way west to Muirkirk. Lanark, seen here, was joined to the CR Glasgow-Carlisle main line by a short branch built without statutory powers and opened for freight in 1854; passengers followed a year later, but it was 1860 before statutory approval was obtained. The main-line junction became triangular in 1864, although the eastbound curve to Carstairs was closed in 1968. Also in 1864 the line towards Muirkirk was opened, initially to Douglas, but reaching its destination in 1873. There was another triangular junction on the outskirts of Lanark, the south-to-east curve of which allowed coal trains from the Douglas area to avoid reversal at Lanark and access the main line directly. Today just the branch to Lanark from the WCML survives; electrified in 1979, it is single track but splits to two platforms in Lanark itself.

Above: This panorama of Ponfeigh station and goods yard, on the Lanark to Muirkirk line, was taken on 8 May 1959 and is looking towards Lanark. The station was situated in the village of Douglas Water, which was also known as Ponfeigh and had developed as a coal-mining community; the river in the valley was also known as the Douglas Water. The name Douglas comes from the Clan Douglas, also known as the House of Douglas, whose original family seat was at nearby Douglas Castle; Prime Minister Sir Alec Douglas-Home was from this family. The village prospered from a large mine opened by the Coltness Iron & Coal Company and known as Douglas Colliery; it had many amenities including a bowling green, which someone appears to be tending at the rear of the station. The passenger service ceased in 1964, but freight continued until 1968, with Ponfeigh becoming a terminus accessed from the Lanark direction; the village is now just a ghost of its former self.

To reach Coalburn after arriving at Ponfeigh on 8 May 1959, the author's father had to hire a taxi, the 5-mile journey costing him 10 shillings. The first railway at Coalburn was the Lesmahagow Railway, authorised in 1854; this was a goods and mineral line promoted by local colliery-owners and the CR, separate accounts being kept in the latter's books until 1860. The railway opened on 1 December 1856 and was single throughout. Passenger traffic started in 1866, but only over the 13 miles and 55 chains from Lesmahagow Junction, Motherwell, as far as Brocketsbrae, the station for Lesmahagow; it was not until 1 November 1891 that the single platform at Coalburn was opened. This view at Coalburn station is looking towards Bankend Colliery, about half a mile further on, and it was here that locomotives ran round their coaches; passengers were not conveyed on this section, which is seen in the first photograph. In the 1850s Muirkirk was one of the principal iron-working towns in Scotland, and the CR had ambitions to reach there and continue westwards to Ayr. The line through Coalburn was extended about 4 miles from Bankend Colliery to Spireslack Colliery and opened in 1888, initially without statutory powers, and in 1896 powers were obtained to extend this a further 4 miles or so to Auldhouseburn, Muirkirk. The Spireslack-Muirkirk section was built, with the inspection train believed to have been hauled by CR single-wheeler No 123; however, this section was never opened to traffic nor was it submitted for Board of Trade approval. The line on to Spireslack closed in the 1950s, Coalburn lost its passenger service in 1965, and freight finished in 1968 when Auchlochan Colliery closed, the 'bing' of which is visible in the panorama. In 1988 Coalburn became home to the largest open-cast coal mine in Western Europe, although it closed in 2003.

Right: Adjacent to the old dual-carriageway A74 and close to its modern equivalent, the M74, is Alton Heights Junction. Four through routes converged here, although only two are still in use in this 1958 view. 'Crab' No 42741 is hauling a loaded coal train from Coalburn to most probably Ross Yards, between Hamilton and Motherwell. Coal was the reason for these railways: the first to arrive, from Motherwell in 1856, was the already closed (1953) and dismantled line in the left foreground, which went on to Bankend Colliery near Coalburn on the Douglas Moors. The line diverging to the left by the signalbox went to Poniel Junction on the Lanark to Muirkirk route, tapping the Douglas area coal deposits, but it had closed in 1954 and now just led a short distance to some sidings; Douglas Castle coal was the selected fuel for CR express locomotives. In the early 1950s there was a choice of four routes for the coal traffic from Alton Heights Junction to Ross Yards – what would Dr Beeching have thought of quadruplication?

Left: About half-way along the 1863-opened single-line Dumfries, Lochmaben & Lockerbie Junction Railway was Shieldhill. Although the station building looks relatively substantial, and once boasted a passing loop, this is quite a remote part of Dumfriesshire near the Ae Water. The bushes in the foreground are beginning to bud as 'Jubilee' No 45588 *Kashmir* makes a scheduled 5-minute photo stop at Shieldhill at 10.02am on Easter Monday 1963 with special train 1X82, during its journey of more than 9 hours from Carlisle to Stranraer. Evidence that this railway came under Caledonian control in 1865 can be seen in the lovely, and now very valuable, CR 'Notice as to Trespass' warning sign to the left of No 45588. The February 1919 'Bradshaw' shows an asymmetric passenger service with three trains to Lockerbie but four in the opposite direction, increasing to five on Wednesdays and Saturdays. Passenger services ended over the branch on 19 May 1952, with complete closure coming 14 years later.

The author's Easter 1963 visit to Dumfries shed found two locomotives in steam outside the depot, which was situated on the east side of the line just south of the station; the bridge in the background carries Annan Road. Dumfries shed (68B), together with Beattock (68D) and Stranraer (68C), had continued to be under the Carlisle District even though Kingmoor shed had been transferred to the English LM Region in February 1958, becoming 12A instead of 68A. In a July 1962 reorganisation both the motive power and traffic departments came in line with each other, Dumfries (67E) and Stranraer (67F) going to the Ayr District, and Beattock (66F) going to Glasgow South. To the right is 'Crab' No 42908, and to the left CR 0-6-0 No 57302, both locally based at Dumfries. The 0-6-0 was still at work here in October 1963, but was withdrawn that month, so did not quite make it into the last batch of working Caley locomotives at the end of November of that year.

Partly visible in the previous photograph, and taken at the same time, are these rows of withdrawn locomotives on the other side of the Annan Road bridge in Dumfries. Although only the number of LMS 2P 4-4-0 No 40670 is visible, it was this locomotive that ended up being the last working member of its class in Scotland. It is believed to have achieved this sad distinction when two classmates were laid up at Hurlford in December 1961. One of the largest concentrations of this class on the LMS had been on the former G&SWR system. When withdrawn at the end of 1962 in the mass culling of Scottish steam, it was the last member of the class to be left in stock anywhere, and is understood to have last worked in May 1962. In fact, the concurrent withdrawals of the last 'Schools' by the SR and Caledonian 4-4-0 in Scotland totally eliminated this wheel arrangement from the BR active stock list, excluding the preserved examples – on 31 December 1949 there had been 1,354 in service. No 56302 and another unidentified class member are both examples of the standard Caledonian Railway shunting tank, developed from the condenser-fitted '29' class of 1895 that worked on the Glasgow Low Level lines. Many of the class ended up with stovepipe chimneys, but not 0-6-0T No 56302, the shape of whose chimney is clearly visible underneath the sacking; one of the last three class survivors, it was another locomotive withdrawn in December 1962 from Dumfries. No 42915, complete with coal rails on its tender, was another end-of-1962 withdrawal from Dumfries, and is a member of the 2-6-0 'Crab' class, the first genuine mixed-traffic engines owned by the LMS, 245 of which were constructed between 1926 and 1932; No 42915 was built at Crewe in 1930. 'J72' 0-6-0T No 68750 follows the same pattern, being a Dumfries locomotive withdrawn in December 1962, although it had been allocated to Aberdeen Kittybrewster throughout the 1950s.

Left: The date is 15 April 1963 and the location Dumfries. 'Black Five' No 44795, allocated to Carlisle Kingmoor (12A) and complete with a small nose snowplough, is pulling away with a freight bound for Stranraer over the 'Port Road'; we will see this locomotive again later this same day on Stranraer shed (67F). The route west was made up of two separate railways: first the Castle Douglas & Dumfries Railway, which was incorporated in 1856 and opened in 1859, and second the Portpatrick Railway, which was authorised in 1857 and by 1861 stretched from Castle Douglas to Stranraer, and to Portpatrick a year later. At one time Portpatrick was regarded as a suitable port for steamer services across to Ireland at Donaghadee, and about £500,000 had been spent by the Government of the day on harbour and protection works. But Portpatrick's vulnerability to strong westerly winds made it impractical for large ships and Stranraer was developed instead; although it meant a longer voyage, Stranraer offered a safe haven out of the north-facing Loch Ryan.

Right: This is Dumfries again, but this time it is Good Friday 1965 and, after a night with relatives nearby, the author and his father were expecting to catch the 8.07am service for a last trip over the 'Port Road' to Stranraer. This train showed a timetabled connection at Dumfries with the overnight 11.40pm sleeper from London Euston, due at Dumfries at 6.58am and including a Restaurant Car onwards from Carlisle, but on this day the sleeper was running very late. The 8.07am normally ran as two trains combined to Castle Douglas, where it split to form Kirkcudbright and Stranraer portions; however, on this day authority decided that it should run as two separate trains from Dumfries, with the Kirkcudbright section departing at 8.07am and the Stranraer section having to wait for the sleeper. So this photograph shows BR Standard Class 4 2-6-0 No 76073, which had been a Dumfries locomotive since newly constructed in October 1956, waiting to leave from one of the bay platforms with just the Kirkcudbright portion.

Right: The reason why 'Jubilee' *Kashmir* is in the up platform at Castle Douglas with a down train for Stranraer is that the Easter 1963 tour train has just arrived back from the Kirkcudbright branch behind No 80023, which is visible in the distance. The railway from Dumfries was double track, but beyond Castle Douglas both lines became single track. The majority of the important Irish traffic ran during the night or early morning and required the main line to be open for the greater part of the day. In addition to the ordinary single-line tablet system, long-section tablet apparatus was installed to reduce the number of exchanging stations when few trains were running. All this came to an end on and from 14 June 1965 when virtually the whole of the main line to Challoch Junction, Dunragit, closed, the exception being a freight-only section at the Dumfries end to Cargenbridge; this lasted until 1994, and the track remained in position for some time after, but now forms part of a walkway and cycleway: the Maxwelltown Railway Path.

Left: Castle Douglas is an important Galloway market town, 19¾ miles from Dumfries and junction for the Kirkcudbright branch. The up (Dumfries) side was once an island platform for convenient interchange of passengers and parcels, etc. The down side used to have the physical track junction, roughly where No 76073 stands in this Good Friday 1965 view; the Kirkcudbright line then headed towards the photographer, together with a platform alongside the cut-away bank, enabling branch passengers to join their waiting service from a Stranraer-bound train on the same curved platform. As befitted an important traffic centre, Castle Douglas used to have goods and carriage sidings, a merchandise depot, engine shed, cattle pens and a turntable. No 76073 will soon head to Kirkcudbright; the author and his father waited here for the delayed Stranraer section to arrive. If the Royal Mail has come to collect post off the train, I wonder if they are aware of today's change of plan!

Right: After waiting at Castle Douglas on 16 April 1965, the Stranraer portion duly arrived behind 'Black Five' No 44995, running late of course. The local passenger service over the full length of the 'Port Line' was rather sparse and consisted of two trains each way daily except Sundays. The author's westbound train was due to pass the eastbound 8.00am from Stranraer at Loch Skerrow, but as No 44995 was behind time the services passed here instead at New Galloway, the next loop east. As everybody waits for BR Standard Class 4 tank engine No 80114 to arrive from the west, the still low sun illuminates the scene at New Galloway station, which was some miles from the pleasant village of that name. On leaving here, No 44995 is faced with about a 4-mile climb up to remote Loch Skerrow on the Galloway Moors; the trackbed of the line is now a foot and cycle path right through to Gatehouse of Fleet station, some 10 miles away. By selecting this remote moorland route, with its consequent lower land prices, rather than the populous coast, construction costs worked out at £7,500 per mile – less than a quarter of the usual figure.

Above: Kirkcudbright (pronounced Kur-koo-bree) was the county town of Kirkcudbrightshire, which in 1975 became part of Dumfries & Galloway; the town has been referred to as 'The Torquay of Scotland'. The branch from Castle Douglas was 11¼ miles long and at the time of this 15 April 1963 rail tour had just one intermediate station at Tarff; Bridge of Dee had closed in 1949 and Castle Douglas St Andrew Street in 1867. No 80023 was used on the branch and had been allocated to Dumfries only the month before. The branch was opened by the Kirkcudbright Railway on 17 February 1864, but was acquired by the G&SWR in 1865, as was the Castle Douglas & Dumfries Railway. In 1922 there were seven passenger trains to Kirkcudbright, but just before closure in May 1965 there were only four. The station was alongside the River Dee and the platform and run-round line had once been under cover, while a quite extensive goods yard filled the area between the station and the waterside. The fine stone engine shed suffered tight clearances, as the notice boards warn, and had closed in 1955; the turntable was of 44ft 6in diameter.

Above: What would today's health & safety regulations have to say about the kilt-wearing enthusiast on the top of the water tank at Loch Skerrow? Scotland had a number of these very remote passing places that were not accessible by road and did not normally appear in the public timetable. Services generally only called at this bleak and wild place for water, to pass another train, or perhaps to drop off an assisting locomotive; the signalbox was continuously manned except for a period on Sundays, and required three signalmen to be stationed here. The line here was opened by the Portpatrick Railway in 1861, becoming the Portpatrick & Wigtownshire Joint Railway following an 1885 Act of Parliament; it was jointly owned by the Caledonian, Glasgow & South Western, London & North Western and Midland railways. The 'Scottish Rambler No 2' joint Easter rail tour of 15 April 1963 behind 'Jubilee' No 45588 has been following the route CR traffic would have taken from Carlisle to Stranraer, the CR owning or jointly owning all the lines except that between Dumfries and Castle Douglas, where it had gained running rights.

Left: Taking over the Easter 1963 rail tour from 'Jubilee' *Kashmir* at Newton Stewart is CR 2F 'Jumbo' 0-6-0 No 57375, for a trip over the old Wigtownshire Railway to Whithorn and Garlieston. Although the enthusiasts had been hoping for No 57375, there had been some doubt; modern Ivatt Class 2 2-6-0 No 46467, which was also at Newton Stewart on this day, had been transferred to Stranraer shed (67F) from Hurlford (67B) in February especially for these branches. Stranraer had done an excellent job cleaning up the veteran 'Jumbo' and it looked superb in the spring sunshine, much to the enjoyment of the tour participants. Dugald Drummond had introduced these locomotives as his 'Standard Goods' design in 1883, and his successors continued the design with slight modification until a total of 244 had been built. The 'Jumbos' remained intact until 1946 and even by the end of 1959 more than half were in stock; this occasion was believed to have been the last ever passenger working by a member of the class.

Left: In all the photographs inherited by the author when his father passed on were two aerial views that appeared to have been taken in the 1920s or 1930s. Neither had any information with them – where they were, who had taken them, and even if they were in the UK. After about ten years the author suddenly realised that this was Newton Stewart and, while the locomotive details cannot be gleaned, it provides an excellent comparison with the modern-day Google Earth view. As for the second aerial photograph, the author has still not been able to identify it, and the picture is now in the mystery photos section of his website – possible identifications would be greatly appreciated.

Left: 'Jumbo' No 57375 has worked down the 19¼ miles of the old Wigtownshire Railway from Newton Stewart to Whithorn on Easter Monday 1963; arrival was due at 3.04pm, and the locomotive has already run round and is ready to depart back to Millisle. Prominent on the tender are two warning flashes for when working under overhead electric wires; there had been cases nationally of footplate staff climbing onto tenders and being seriously injured or worse. The village of Whithorn lies at the southern end of The Machars, a broad peninsula projecting south into the Irish Sea, and Whithorn station was the most southerly in Scotland; it had taken this title from Kirkcudbright when the WR opened. Behind us in this view was the Whithorn Creamery, which had opened in 1903 and generated much traffic for the railway. In February 1919 there were four passenger trains daily from Newton Stewart to Whithorn, with three in the opposite direction, and none on Sundays. In the pre-Grouping era, the Caledonian Railway ran through carriages to Whithorn from Edinburgh Princes Street via Lockerbie and Dumfries. Passenger services ceased on 25 September 1950, but freight carried on until October 1964, thrice-weekly at the end; closure passed the title of the most southerly station back to Kirkcudbright.

Right: From Whithorn the tour went north to Millisle, junction for one of the more obscure Scottish branch lines, that to Garlieston. Normal passenger coaching stock was prohibited by this time, so tour participants had to decant into these empty freight wagons behind 'Jumbo' No 57375 to traverse the Garlieston branch, the scheduled departure time from Millisle being 3.55pm. It was a good job the weather had been excellent all day, but it is another example of a procedure that would not be tolerated in today's health-&-safety-conscious world. The Wigtownshire Railway amalgamated with the Portpatrick Railway to become the Portpatrick & Wigtownshire Joint Railway in 1885. For this new company's Stranraer to Castle Douglas main line locomotives were provided in equal number by the CR and the G&SWR, but not on the old Wigtownshire Railway tracks. For working between Newton Stewart and Whithorn engines were hired in at an hourly rate, and in 1911 this was from the G&SWR.

Right: No 57375 stands in the afternoon sunshine at Garlieston Harbour on 15 April 1963. The WR opened from Newton Stewart to Wigtown for goods traffic on 3 March 1875 and thence to Millisle five months later. From Millisle a mile-long tramway was authorised to Garlieston (or Garliestown, as it was prior to 1909) by the 1872 Wigtownshire Railway Act. However, a branch railway was built instead, opening on 3 April 1876, and a Parliamentary Bill of 1877 retrospectively legalised this. The branch closed to regular passenger services as long ago as 1 March 1903, but freight carried on for more than 60 years longer before ceasing in 1964, latterly running as required. Occasional boat excursions were run from Garlieston Harbour to the Isle of Man up to 1935, and trains ran to here in connection with them. No 57375 remained in the running stock at Stranraer for most of 1963 although was seldom used, though it made at least one more trip along the WR on 21 August. On 29 November of that year the last eight Caley locomotives left in stock were simultaneously withdrawn, including No 57375.

Left: On their journey west from Dumfries to Stranraer on Good Friday 1965 the author and his father got off the morning stopping service at Dunragit. Although 'Black Five' No 44995 arrived late, there was plenty of time to look around this country station before catching the 11.40am DMU service from Glasgow St Enoch for the remaining 5½ miles to Stranraer Town. At this time Dunragit was served by four trains daily except Sundays to and from Stranraer, two each way using the Glasgow line and the other two using the Dumfries route; on Saturdays only there was an extra service to Stranraer from Glasgow at 11.45pm. No 44995 is now for the first time since Castle Douglas on double track as far as the next station at Castle Kennedy. This work was done during the Second World War because of extra traffic, especially that for Cairn Point on the Cairnryan Military Railway, which was seen as an alternative to Liverpool and Glasgow should they be badly damaged by bombing.

Left: These two views show Dunragit station as it was on Friday 16 April 1965. The line from Dumfries had opened in 1861, and a possible source of further business was the 1865 Act authorising the Girvan & Portpatrick Joint Railway, designed to bring Irish traffic from the west of Scotland to a junction near East Challoch farmstead, just east of Dunragit. No immediate action was taken and the G&PJR had its powers revived by an Act of 1870, eventually opening in 1877, but the line had many problems over its 32 miles from Girvan. Floods swept away bridges and embankments, the gradients were severe, including a stretch of some 1 in 55 for 3¾ miles, and the line ran through bleak countryside; for much of its length there was scarcely a sign of life, and it therefore had to rely on through traffic if it was to pay. The costs of construction, at £532,900 17s 11d, ended up ridiculously disproportionate to the possible returns of the traffic, and the line was in difficulties from the beginning. It was worked by the G&SWR at cost price, but the G&PJR still could not make a profit, and the line was closed altogether more than once. A private syndicate of London capitalists bought it for £155,000 in 1887 and altered the name to the Ayrshire & Wigtownshire Railway; it was subsequently purchased by the G&SWR in 1892 for £235,000. The separate routes from Dumfries and Girvan joined at Challoch Junction, where there used to be a signalbox that closed in 1939, replaced with motor points controlled from Dunragit, about a mile to the west. Dunragit station closed with the 'Port Line' in June 1965, despite the line north to Glasgow remaining open; it is today just a passing place. Nowadays passengers must travel from Dumfries to Stranraer via Kilmarnock, not of course via the 'Port Line'; this is more than 60 miles longer and approaching double the old distance; initially though services such as the overnight train from London were operated via Annbank.

At the rear of Dunragit yard on the same day was this six-wheel veteran, and thanks to the help of Stuart Rankin, the Glasgow & South Western Railway Association's archivist, the author has been given some details of it, including the accompanying 7mm/ft scale drawing. It is one of a series of 114 similar passenger brake vans (PBVs) built to the design of James Manson, the G&SWR Locomotive Superintendent, between 1894 and 1910. They were gas-lit with distinctive peaked-shaped roof ventilators, still present in 1965 as the photograph shows. Originally it would have been painted in the company's maroon livery, lined and lettered in gold, there would have been seats and lookouts (still present) for the guard, and a coal-fired stove. When new it would have been used on the G&SWR's express trains between Glasgow and Carlisle or Stranraer, so is likely to be no stranger to Dunragit. The G&SWR used the automatic vacuum brake; however, a number of other companies such as the Caledonian used the Westinghouse automatic air brake, so some of this series of PBVs were dual-fitted for through working. These vehicles had a 31-foot underframe with a tare weight of 13 tons, and by 1910 were the last six-wheelers built by the G&SWR. Development from short four-wheeled coaches to six-wheeled ones like this vehicle improved the ride, but by modern standards they were still uncomfortable. Nevertheless, six-wheeled (and some four-wheeled) carriages remained in use on branch-line and workmen's trains into the 1930s. There was some alteration to the woodwork in LMS days; in this example the panelling was replaced by matchboarding. A number, including this one, were transferred to service stock as Pooley & Sons weighing machine vans to go around the system calibrating machines, the vehicle being based at No 14 siding in Buchanan Street Goods Station, Glasgow.

GLASGOW AND SOUTH WESTERN RAILWAY

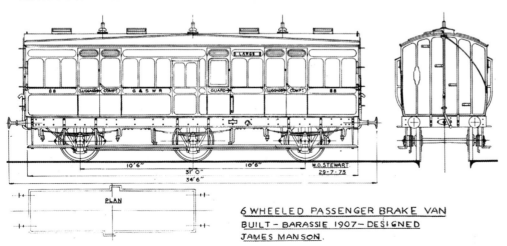

6 WHEELED PASSENGER BRAKE VAN
BUILT - BARASSIE 1907 - DESIGNED
JAMES MANSON.

Right: 'Jubilee' No 45588 *Kashmir* bathes in the evening sunshine at Stranraer Town station after arriving with the 'Scottish Rambler' Easter 1963 tour. It has been a long day for *Kashmir*, as it is now about 6.15pm and departure from Carlisle had been at 9.00am, although other motive power was used on some of the branches. This station had originally been just plain Stranraer, becoming Stranraer Town in 1953; today the name Stranraer is used for what was Stranraer Harbour station. By this time Stranraer Town was a terminus, but until 6 February 1950 the passenger service continued west to Portpatrick, after which freight carried on to the single intermediate station of Colfin until 1 April 1959, primarily for Colfin Creamery. Passenger services continued on at Stranraer Town station after closure of the 'Port Road' in 1965 until March 1966; since then all passenger traffic, both local and Irish, uses what was Stranraer Harbour station. Just visible to the right of the locomotive is Stranraer Harbour Junction signalbox.

Left: There is plenty of activity in this view, looking east from the footbridge at Stranraer Town station on 16 April 1965. The DMU had worked down to the Harbour station from Glasgow as the 11.25am 'Stranraer-Larne Boat Train' and is now waiting for its 4.25pm return to St Enoch. It is one of the Swindon-built Inter-City units with a half-cab and central gangway connection, later Class 126, that were introduced to this route in the summer of 1959. 'Black Five' No 44995 is in the bay waiting for its 3.50pm departure back to Dumfries. The area between the Town station and the single-line branch to the Harbour station was occupied by extensive sidings and the engine shed complex. At one time there were separate shed facilities for the CR and G&SWR, each having its own locomotive foreman and staff. Above the first coach of the Dumfries train can be seen the lightly built 25-ton bucket hoist coaler installed in 1937; referred to as the 'Stranraer type', it was used at LMS secondary depots.

Left: Easter 1963 at Stranraer shed (67F) finds the evening sun still shining. On the far right is 'Black Five' No 44795 from Carlisle Kingmoor (12A), complete with snowplough; we have already seen this locomotive earlier the same day at Dumfries, heading a westbound freight. In the middle is Ivatt Class 2 2-6-0 No 46467 complete with its 67F shed code, and again this had been seen earlier in the day at Newton Stewart, but not so far in this book; it was a recent replacement for the Caledonian 'Jumbos' working the weight-restricted Wigtownshire Railway lines to Whithorn and Garlieston. On the left is 'Clan' Pacific No 72006 *Clan Mackenzie*; at this time only five of the 'Clans' were still in service, and all were based at Carlisle Kingmoor. These last two locomotives are outside the joint shed, with the track to the right of No 44795 leading to the Girvan shed. No 72006 achieved a strange distinction in August 1964 by incorrectly acquiring the yellow diagonal cabside stripe that denoted locomotives banned from working south from Crewe under electrified lines.

Right: Two years later at Stranraer shed (67F), this time it is a dull day. The tall building is the original Portpatrick Railway Works, which still had an overhead crane inside. On the left is 'Black Five' No 44995, allocated to Dumfries (67E), which had hauled the author's morning train that day from Castle Douglas to Stranraer. No 44995 remained at Dumfries until April 1966, when the shed lost its steam allocation; it was then transferred to Glasgow Corkerhill (67A). In the background is BR Standard Class 5 No 73057; although looking different from a 'Black Five', it is in fact a development of this numerous LMS class. Corkerhill had a long association with the BR Standard Class 5s and received ten brand-new ones between May 1955 and February 1956; others arrived later, including No 73057, which came from Polmadie (66A) in June 1964. The class began to monopolise the Stranraer line duties from Corkerhill, including the 8.55am, 12.30pm and 9.00pm 'Irishman' boat train from Glasgow St Enoch, together with the return workings. Freight duties included the 1.00am 'College' goods to Stranraer and the return 'Milk'.

Left: Stranraer Harbour is seen on Good Friday, 16 April 1965, with the 1.30pm 'Larne-Stranraer Boat Train' leaving on its 100¾-mile journey to Glasgow St Enoch, due to arrive there at 4.15pm with a first stop at Girvan. The boat had left Larne at 11.00am following the arrival of the 10.05am connecting train from Belfast York Road, the passage across the North Channel taking 2¼ hours. The return sailing was at 2.30pm, and just approaching the queue for this is Mark 1 Ford Cortina AYS 219B, a Glasgow plate. The branch down to Stranraer Harbour was opened in 1862, and in 1874 Portpatrick Harbour was formally abandoned by Act of Parliament. The old harbour at Stranraer was not suitable for heavy draught vehicles, but this railway pier goes out sufficiently to allow large vessels to come alongside at all states of the tide. The pier carried two rail lines, a public road and an enclosed cattle path, as a considerable cattle traffic passed this way. The ferry service was operated by the TSS *Caledonian Princess* (3,630 tons), built by William Denny & Brothers of Dumbarton and launched on Wednesday 5 April 1961. It was a dual-purpose ship accommodating 1,400 passengers with luxury sleeping cabins for 170; it had stabilisers and space for more than 100 cars, with ramp-loading that allowed drive-on and drive-off via an on-board turntable. After later spending many years on the Tyne at Newcastle as a nightclub, where the turntable was allegedly used as a revolving dance floor, it was reported being towed to Aliaga, Turkey, for demolition in August 2008.

Left: Great North of Scotland Railway No 49 *Gordon Highlander* and Highland Railway No 103 make a fine sight as they back on to the 'Scottish Rambler' tour at Stranraer on 15 April 1963, their tenders stacked high with coal for the just less than 3-hour journey to Glasgow St Enoch, a route that is mostly still open today. However, the 'Port Road' to Dumfries closed from 14 June 1965, and was still entirely steam-operated even then, by far the longest line still so operated throughout Scotland. The last weeks of the 'Port Road' were not devoid of interest. On Sunday 16 May three TA specials were run to Woodburn, Northumberland, with the three Class 6 locomotives – No 45573 *Newfoundland*, No 72006 *Clan Mackenzie* and No 72008 *Clan Macleod* – running light coupled from Kingmoor to Stranraer. The three trains returned on Sunday 30 May, this time with three 'Clans'. The previous day two more military specials were run to Stranraer with 'Clans'.

The engine shed at Kilmarnock suffered from a lack of capacity for the growing traffic, with virtually no room for expansion, so in 1873 the G&SWR decided to move to a greenfield site about 2 miles away at Hurlford, seen here during Easter 1963. Primarily a freight depot for the coal and minerals in the area, it suffered during the Great Depression when it was said that no footplate-grade staff were recruited for 19 years. However, during February 1963 Ayr had become a central collection point for coal shipments to power stations in the South of England and Northern Ireland; coal was moving 24 hours a day and sheds like Hurlford were hard-pressed to meet the increased traffic. Nevertheless, it was common to see lines of silent steam locomotives either stored or withdrawn from service; Hurlford had 25 on 13 October 1962 and 12 on 5 June 1963. LMS 2P 4-4-0 No 40665 was there on both occasions with its Hurlford name just visible on the buffer beam. When the electric 'Blue Train' service commenced along the north bank of the Clyde on 7 November 1960, some of the displaced Gresley 'V1' and 'V3' three-cylinder 2-6-2Ts were reallocated to Hurlford. However, when the electric service was withdrawn that December following a series of transformer explosions, all the 2-6-2Ts bar one were quickly returned for the hastily reintroduced steam service. Following restoration of the 'Blue Trains', surplus 'V1s' and 'V3s' again ended up at Hurlford, and it was expected that complete withdrawal of the remaining LMS 2P 4-4-0s would follow. Two of the 2-6-2Ts can be seen along the row of forlorn locomotives. The two CR 0-6-0s are Nos 57359 and 57249, both of which were noted stored here on 19 March 1962 together with five of the Gresley 2-6-2Ts.

Right: On 10 April 1966 the 'Scottish Rambler No 5' rail tour approaches Mauchline behind 'B1' No 61342 on its way from Ayr to Muirkirk. The line in the foreground is the Glasgow & South Western main line from Glasgow to Carlisle. The G&SWR became the third largest in Scotland and was formed by an amalgamation of earlier railways in 1850, the same time that the Glasgow to Carlisle line was completed. Traffic difficulties with the Glasgow to London West Coast companies restricted through working, and the G&SWR welcomed the opening of the Midland Railway line from Settle to Carlisle. Immediately the two companies started running through expresses between Glasgow St Enoch and London St Pancras and, although the route was slower, luxurious carriages were used. The daytime train was given the name 'The Thames-Clyde Express' by the LMS in 1927, but by the winter 1964 timetable Glasgow Central was being used in preference to St Enoch, and arrival at Euston an hour earlier was promoted by changing at Carlisle.

Left: Mauchline station is seen on Saturday 9 May 1959, with LMS 4-4-0 No 40574 at the head of the 'Burns Country' rail tour, although originally a CR 3F 0-6-0 was due to haul the train. The station is 9½ miles south of Kilmarnock on the G&SWR main line from Glasgow to Carlisle, and was a junction for the line west to Annbank and Ayr, the route that has just been followed by No 40574. It was also the junction station for the short branch to Catrine, which opened in 1903 and left the main line some 2 miles south of Mauchline at Brackenhill Junction; it lost its passenger service in 1943 and freight in 1964, and is another line that No 40574 will be traversing today. Between Mauchline and Brackenhill Junction is Ballochmyle Viaduct, constructed between 1846 and 1848; it had the world's largest masonry span arch when built, and even today is the highest extant railway viaduct in Britain.

Left: The 'Scottish Rambler No 5' tour was due to arrive here at Muirkirk at 5.02pm on Sunday 10 April 1966. After running round its train in 10 minutes, departure back to Glasgow Central was via Lugton and the Giffen branch. Muirkirk, at a height of 720 feet, has been described as one of the bleakest towns in Scotland, but close by were deposits of coal, ironstone and limestone. The Industrial Revolution created a demand for these materials and the result was the establishment of the Muirkirk Iron Company in 1787. The first railway to the outside world came with the opening of a branch from Auchinleck in 1848, and eventually there were four separate routes to the town, although as described earlier in this book, that from Coalburn was never opened to through traffic. The works closed in 1923 following a strike in which the furnaces cooled with the iron inside them. Muirkirk lost its final passenger services in 1964, with freight ceasing five years later.

Right: LMS 2P 4-4-0 No 40574 stands at Cumnock A&C station on 9 May 1959, hauling the Stephenson Locomotive Society's 'Burns Country' rail tour back from Muirkirk to Ayr. When the LMS was created at the Grouping by the amalgamation of existing railway companies, a policy of what has been described as 'Midlandisation' was followed, and large-scale building of pure old Midland Railway 'small engine' designs was pursued. These 4-4-0s were introduced in 1928, but were a post-Grouping development of the MR version that had originated in Victorian times; 138 locomotives were built up to 1932. The locomotives had a 'constipated' front end with undersized valves and short-travel Stephenson's gear, which gave a very uninspiring performance and were totally inferior to Wainwright's South Eastern & Chatham Railway 4-4-0s, which could haul heavy continental expresses. However, though their performance was indifferent, their simple and robust construction in relation to their usually light duties produced the lowest average repair costs in pence per mile of any LMS passenger type.

Four G&SWR routes converged here at Annbank. No 40574 is hauling the SLS tour to which the ticket relates and has arrived from Ayr via Auchincruive; it will continue eastwards to Mauchline via Tarbolton on a route that opened in 1870. In 1872 a line was opened south from Annbank to Cronberry via Cumnock, where it joined the existing railway to Muirkirk. The fourth line left the Ayr route west of Annbank at Mossblown Junction to join the Ayr to Glasgow line near where Prestwick International Airport is today; this opened in 1892. The February 1919 'Bradshaw' shows five passenger trains each way between Ayr and Annbank, three of which carried on along the Tarbolton line and two along that to Cumnock and Muirkirk. Annbank lost its passenger services on 10 September 1951, but freight continues; the Cumnock line is open to the site of Killoch Colliery via a new 1959 connection, and the Ayr to Mauchline line handles coal trains. Initially, after closure of the 'Port Road' in 1965, the 'Northern Irishman' Sleeping Car service (often 'Britannia'-hauled) from London Euston to Stranraer was routed via Annbank.

It is lunchtime at Ayr station on Sunday 10 April 1966, and locally based 'Black Five' No 44788 is on station pilot duties; note that it has tablet-catching apparatus on its cab side for use on suitably equipped single lines such as that to Stranraer. The Glasgow, Paisley, Kilmarnock & Ayr Railway arrived in the town at its North Side station as early as 1839. When the Ayr & Dalmellington Railway opened in 1856 it built Townhead station on the south side of the town; North Side was closed the following year. The station seen here is the third to be named Ayr; it was opened by the G&SWR on 12 January 1886 and is some 300 yards south of Townhead, which closed on the same day. Things are very different here nowadays; in 1986 the Glasgow services were electrified, with the overhead wires continuing south of the station to Townhead EMU sidings, used for storage and maintenance. The service is popular, Ayr station attracting about 1.4 million passengers annually.

Right: A wet day at Ayr in 1960 finds Fairburn 2-6-4T No 42122 complete with local 67C shed plate. This class was a development of its Stanier predecessor and added to the already more than 300 2-6-4Ts owned by the LMS. The coupled wheelbase was reduced by 14 inches, which both decreased the total weight and allowed 5-chain-radius curves to be negotiated instead of 6, giving extended route availability. As with the 'Black Fives', construction continued well into BR days, and the class outran the logical number series. Despite being an LMS design, 41 of the class were built at Brighton for use on the Southern Region. Behind No 42122 and partly obscured by steam is the Station Hotel, which was opened by the G&SWR in June 1866. On nationalisation it became part of British Transport Hotels, but was sold in 1951; at present it is owned by Swallow Hotels and has retained almost all of its original features inside and out.

Eleven years after BR steam came to an end in Scotland, and ten years after BR main-line steam was eliminated nationally, it was still possible to see steam in commercial revenue-earning service such as here at Waterside Colliery, near Dalmellington, Ayrshire, in May 1978. The Waterside system had boasted a main line with branches, and in this delightfully rural picture NCB No 24, built locally by Andrew Barclay of Kilmarnock in 1953 (works number 2235) and fitted with a Giesl ejector, is hard at work.

The locomotive had been delivered as No 8 but was renumbered in 1963; the Giesl ejector chimney was fitted to improve steaming and to allow poor-quality coal to be used. No 24 has a tender wagon coupled to it for topping up the locomotive during the shift. The area is now the site of the Scottish Industrial Railway Centre, and some of the engines that worked locally are still there – not No 24, however, which is on the Bo'ness & Kinniel Railway.

Right: The railway from Ayr reached a terminus at Girvan via Maybole in May 1860. When the line was extended south in 1877 over what became known as the 'Stranraer Road', a new but rather primitive through Girvan station was established; it dealt only with the Stranraer services, and the old station continued in use for terminating trains until 1893, by which time the new station had been rebuilt to cope with all the passenger traffic. From then on the old station became the freight depot for Girvan, and this is where 'B1' No 61342 is standing on 10 April 1966 with the 'Scottish Rambler No 5' tour, awaiting departure back to Ayr. The new Girvan station, which is still open today, could be very busy, as on Glasgow Fair Friday 1931, when 44 southbound trains were dealt with, 30 of which terminated at Girvan, together with 42 northbound, and all at two short platforms on a curve and steep gradient.

Left: The Branch Line Society's 'Scottish Rambler No 5' tour of Sunday 10 April 1966, with 'B1' No 61342 in charge, has just left Girvan Goods and is climbing the 1 in 72 between Killochan and Dailly on its way to Ayr, a freely downloadable tape-recording of which can be heard on the author's website (www.michaelclemensrailways.co.uk) by clicking on the 'Sound Bites' section. The railway here had been built by the Maybole & Girvan Railway and opened in 1860; it was originally single track from Dalrymple, but the entire section through to Girvan had been doubled by 1894. This area has a strangely isolated coalfield that was in production as long ago as the 15th century, and in the 1830s produced around 20,000 tons annually. One of the coal measures was accidentally set alight in Victorian times, and it was still possible to see smoke rising through fissures from passing trains in the 1930s; not surprisingly, subsidence was a problem for the railway. Nowadays the line here is single track with a passing loop at Kilkerran.

Easter Monday, 15 April 1963, had been a superb day. There had been plenty to see since leaving Carlisle at 9.00am and the sun shone all the time. We were now on our way back to Glasgow in the evening sunshine, with the first photograph showing the view looking north at Glenwhilly, between Stranraer and Girvan, surrounded by the bleak moorland that caused considerable difficulty during construction of the line. The bogs around here created problems reminiscent of those experienced decades before at the Liverpool & Manchester Railway's crossing of Chat Moss, by persistently swallowing material. Eventually the railway had to be supported on a raft of hurdles, straw, wool and brushwood.

The sun had almost disappeared in the second photograph at Barrhill station, some 8½ miles north of Glenwhilly, and it seems a fitting image with which to conclude this book. As Great North of Scotland Railway No 49 *Gordon Highlander* takes on water, with Highland Railway No 103 coupled in front, the pair (both restored to working order in 1959) took advantage of their five-minute scheduled stop here from 7.08pm to pass the 5.10pm Glasgow to Stranraer service. However, things were changing fast on the railways of Britain; many of the places visited on this day, and indeed shown throughout this book, are no longer on the railway map, while BR main-line steam came to an end well over four decades ago. Barrhill station is still open though, as a passing loop on the 50+ miles of single track from Dalrymple Junction, Ayr, to Stranraer. Moreover, both locomotives are still in existence – this scene could perhaps even be recreated some day.